Hope for the Heart
Christ's Response for Me

By

Julianne Pickle

Hope for the Heart

Christ's Response for Me

"Grow in grace, and in the knowledge of
our Lord and Savior Jesus Christ."
II Peter 3:18

Biblical Response Therapy®, simplified

Julianne Pickle

TEACH Services, Inc.
P U B L I S H I N G
www.TEACHServices.com • (800) 367-1844

World rights reserved. This book or any portion thereof may not be copied or reproduced in any form or manner whatever, except as provided by law, without the written permission of the publisher, except by a reviewer who may quote brief passages in a review.

The author assumes full responsibility for the accuracy of all facts and quotations as cited in this book. The opinions expressed in this book are the author's personal views and interpretations, and do not necessarily reflect those of the publisher.

This book is provided with the understanding that the publisher is not engaged in giving spiritual, legal, medical, or other professional advice. If authoritative advice is needed, the reader should seek the counsel of a competent professional.

The editors of this book have capitalized the pronouns referring to God in the Bible references cited. All scripture references are taken from the King James Version of the Bible unless otherwise stated.

References marked (NKJV) are taken from the New King James Version of the Bible. ©Thomas Nelson Publishers.

Copyright © 2018 Julianne Pickle

Copyright © 2018 TEACH Services, Inc.

ISBN-13: 978-1-4796-0989-5 (Paperback)

ISBN-13: 978-1-4796-0990-1 (ePub)

Library of Congress Control Number: 2018907577

Image Credits: (www.bigstockphoto.com) Ch.1-robodread; Ch.2-MIA Studio; Ch.3-Sinisa Botas; Ch.4-artitcom; Ch.5-Nik_Sorokin; Ch.6-TongPoon; Ch.7-Flynt; Ch.8-mypokcik; Ch.9-artitcom; Ch.10-BillionPhotos.com; Ch.11-Orla; Ch.12-Orla; Ch.13-Slaan; Ch.14-InesBazdar; Ch.15-HighwayStarz; Ch.16-Wordley Calvo Stock; Ch.17-Waldemarus; Ch.18-argus456; Ch.19-pinock; Ch.20-Gino Santa Maria; Ch.21-paul Shuang; Ch.22-VelourRouge; Ch.23-gracel; Ch.24-BillionPhotos.com; Ch.25-Koldunov; Ch.26-ajn; Ch.27-jamesteoh; Ch.28-Wayhome Studio; Ch.29-chalabala; Ch.30-gunnar3000

Credits

These studies are adapted and simplified from the thoughtfully prepared book, ***Biblical Response Therapy*®**, by Dan Gabbert, which contains a wealth of helpful material. It is available from the following source.

Black Hills Health and Education Center

Web: http://1ref.us/ni

Phone: http://1ref.us/nh

NOTICE: Please be respectful of the work that went into this book, and purchase additional copies instead of reproducing them. Thank you!

God has provided, in His Word,
a way for humanity to find forgiveness and healing
from the damage that sin has caused
in our hearts and minds.
Through understanding and applying the principles
found in God's word,
we can receive freedom.
We can receive the peace Christ died to give us.

Contents

The Laws of the Mind. 9
Understanding and Applying Scripture 14
Priceless Treasures 16
The Purpose for Living. 19
Can God be Trusted?. 22
Why is There Evil and Misery? 26
Power To Choose. 29
Faith at Work. 32
The Gift of Grace 35
Take Your Conscience to School 38
Guilty 41
My Way. 45
The Power of the Plan 48
He Didn't Treat Me Nicely! 51
Forgive? But She …!. 54
Problems—Why? Part 1 57
Problems—Why? Part 2 61
Responding to Difficulties God's Way Part 1: The Crisis. 65
Responding to Difficulties God's Way Part 2: The Long Term 70
To Be Like Jesus 75
Looking to Jesus 79
Anger 82
Don't Be Afraid. 87
Fear Fighting Formula 92
I'm Good 95
When Life Seems Overwhelming 98
God's Plan for Victory 102
Prayer. 107

Be Thankful Still 111
Life's Cup. 114
Bibliography. 117

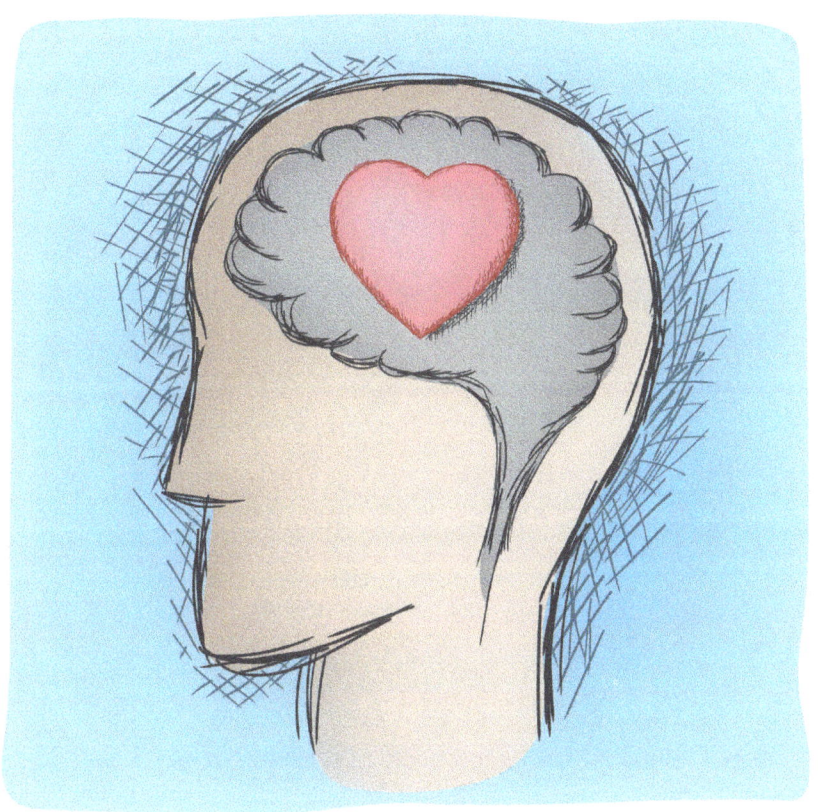

The Laws of the Mind
Healing the Heart of the Matter

"Keep thy heart with all diligence; for out of it are the issues of life"
(Proverbs 4:23).

Our mind is a wonderful thing! What happens between our ears affects every part of our daily lives. There are laws (principles) to preserve our minds in the best of health. To co-operate with these laws, we have to contend against our selfish natures and the enemy of all good. When on the battlefield of our mind we must do warfare over our thoughts and attitudes; we need the help of Heaven. The results are well worth the effort.

Let's look at the first law.

Law #1

- *John 15:5— "Without Me ye can do _____."*

Our efforts may make the outside of our lives look good, but to change the heart, we must have the help of Heaven. We must have the power of Christ working in our hearts. *(see Psalm 139:23, 24; Ezekiel 36:26, 27; Philippians 4:13, 19)*

Daily ask God for that new heart that only He can give.
- *II Corinthians 5:17— "Therefore if any man be in Christ, he is a new creature: old things are passed away; behold, all things are become new." (see also Ephesians 4:22–24)*

There is no true excellence of character apart from Jesus.
- *John 1:4— "In Him was _____; and the life was the _____ of men." (see also Romans 7:18)*
- *Psalm 40:1, 2— "I waited patiently for the Lord; and He inclined unto me, and heard my cry. He brought me _____ also out of an horrible pit, out of the miry clay, and set my feet upon a rock, and _____ my goings." (see also Isaiah 64:6; Jeremiah 10:23; 13:23; I Corinthians 15:57; Romans 8:1–4; Ephesians 2:10)*

The battle is a cooperative effort. Here's the next part we do together.

Law #2

- *Proverbs 23:7— "For as he _____ in his heart, so is he."*

You are what you think. Watch those thoughts, because thoughts become attitudes and feelings. Words and responses follow close behind.

If you find your behavior out of line, go to the source—challenge your thinking. Talk to God about your thoughts, and His promises regarding them. Make promises like *II Corinthians 10:3–5*, personal, with thankfulness, like this:

"Thank You Lord, that though I walk in the flesh, I need not war in my own strength. Thank You that my weapons aren't carnal, but mighty through Jesus to the pulling down of strong holds. Thank You for casting down my imaginations, and every high thing that exalts itself against the knowledge of You. Thank You for helping to bring my every thought to the obedience of Christ."

As you go about your duties, keep praying to God about your thoughts.

- *Proverbs 4:23—* *"Keep thy heart [mind] with all _____, for out of it are the issues of life."*

Here's another principle.

Law #3

- *Galatians 6:7—* *"_____ a man soweth, that shall he also reap."*

What we plant in the garden, that's what we harvest. Our minds work similarly. If you sow false or negative thoughts, you reap negative feelings and negative results throughout the whole body. If you sow true or positive thoughts, you will reap not only positive feelings, but positive words, attitudes, and actions.

This helps us understand why the next principle is important.

Law #4

- *II Corinthians 3:18—* *"We all," [by] "beholding ... are _____ into the same image."*

Whatever we give our attention to, changes us. This principle works not only for good things, but also for bad. It includes more than just what our eyes see. What our other senses (like our ears) take in, affects our thoughts, feelings, and responses to life, too. So, choosing what is good will bring such blessings. *(see I Corinthians 15:33; Proverbs 13:20)*

Here is a verse to show us the best things to pay attention to—to behold.

- *Philippians 4:8—* *"Finally, brethren [and sisters], whatsoever things are _____, whatsoever things are _____, whatsoever things are _____, whatsoever things are _____, whatsoever things are _____, whatsoever things are of _____ report, if there be any _____, and if there be any _____, think on these things."*

We must persistently put good things in the mind if we want it to work in a healthy way. The Bible is a trustworthy guide to show us what is good for all areas of life.

- *II Timothy 3:16, 17— "_____ scripture is given by inspiration of God, and is profitable [good] for doctrine, for reproof, for correction, for instruction in righteousness: that the man of God may be perfect, thoroughly furnished unto all good works."*

Here is the next law.

Law #5

- *Romans 12:21—"Be not overcome of evil, but _____ evil with good."*

If you want to get rid of something bad, replace it with something good. Don't leave a void, or the bad will come back, and likely it will be even worse than before. This works with our thoughts, habits, and responses, too. *(see Luke 11:23–26; II Peter 2:20)*

* * * * * * *

What the Bible asks us to do can be accomplished only in the strength Heaven provides. For every battle of the mind, seek help from above. *(see John 15:5; Philippians 4:13)*

- *Hebrews 4:14–16— "Seeing then that we have a great high priest, that is passed into the heavens, Jesus the Son of God, let us hold fast our profession. For we have not an high priest which cannot be touched with the feeling of our infirmities; but was in _____ points tempted like as we are, yet without sin. Let us therefore come _____ unto the throne of grace, that we may obtain mercy, and find grace to help in time of need."*

- *Romans 8:32— "He that spared not His own Son, but delivered Him up for us all, how shall He not with Him also _____ give us all things?"*

- *I Thessalonians 5:24— "_____ is He that calleth you, who also will do it."*

God has called us to be like Him in our thoughts and feelings, and in our words and responses to those around us. He alone can help us throw out the bad, and replace it with the good. We can't save ourselves.

So, connect with Heaven, watch your thoughts, be careful what you sow, give your mind wholesome input (keep focused on the positive things), and overcome evil with good.

Got it? Keep at it. ☺

Be a Sleuth

What parts of our lifestyles also affect our mental health? Exercise? Fresh air? Diet? TV? Alcohol? Tobacco? Caffeine? Enough rest? Drugs? Relationships? Trust in God? Clutter? Noise? Music? More?

Understanding and Applying Scripture

"Study to shew thyself approved unto God, a workman that needeth not to be ashamed, rightly dividing the word of truth" (II Timothy 2:15).

Have you heard about the method of Bible study that Jesus taught His followers? We are told about it in the story of the two men on the road to Emmaus. They were walking along, talking about the sad crucifixion weekend. They didn't yet believe that Jesus had risen. A stranger joined them, and they sadly told him all about it. The "stranger" was Jesus. This is how He explained the difficulty to them.

- *Luke 24:27— "And beginning at Moses and all the prophets, He expounded unto them in _____ the scriptures the things concerning Himself."*

Jesus' method is great for understanding the Bible. It gives an excellent, all-over view of what the Bible teaches. It is a great method for understanding doctrine, prophecy, and many other topics.

Here's how.
1. Pray for guidance from the Holy Spirit.
2. Choose a topic and think of key words about the topic.

a) Look up in a concordance every place where those words are mentioned in the Bible.
   b) Compare it all.

This method helps explain the big picture, and gives us lots of details.

Here is also a more devotional method that teaches us about God's character and helps us look victoriously to Jesus. *(see Hebrews 12:2, 3; Isaiah 45:22; John 5:39)*

1. Ask God to send the Holy Spirit to help you understand.
2. Choose a short passage of Scripture (perhaps from the Gospels).
3. Ask these questions:
   a) What does this say about God?
   b) What does this say about me?
   c) What does this say about God's plan for me now?

Keep everything in balance (This method is not suited for *every* passage of Scripture). Ask God to show you more about Jesus, and make you like Him.

- *John 8:32—* "And ye shall know the truth, and the truth shall make you _____."

- *I Thessalonians 5:24—* "_____ is He that calleth you, who also will _____."

Keep looking to Jesus!

Be a Sleuth

How essential is daily Bible study and prayer? Of what benefit is knowledge of the Bible? How should Bible knowledge affect our Christian experience and daily living? Are there things or activities that make Bible study seem boring to us or to our families? Should we keep doing those things?

Priceless Treasures

"In this was manifested the love of God toward us, because that God sent His only begotten Son into the world, that we might live through Him" (I John 4:9).

    You are Jesus' priceless treasure! Have you considered the price He paid for you? He knew of you long before you were born and has loved you forever. Even if you feel scratched and covered in mud, to Him, you are still His priceless treasure. Yes, you, and all the rest of humanity, for whom He gave His precious life.

    You *are* Jesus' priceless treasure. Look what kind of God He is.
- *I John 4:8—* "God is _____."

Here is more about Him.
- *Exodus 34:6—* "The Lord God, _____ and _____, _____, and abundant in _____ and _____."

This Great God knew about you before you were born.
- *Jeremiah 1:5— "Before I formed thee in the belly I _____ thee." (see also Psalm 139:16)*

He truly has loved you forever!
- *Jeremiah 31:3— "Yea, I have loved thee with an _____ love: therefore with lovingkindness have I drawn thee."*

Look what kind of value God the Father has placed on you.
- *John 3:16— "For God so _____ the world, that He gave his only begotten Son, that whosoever believeth in Him should not perish, but have everlasting life."*

The life of Jesus, the Creator, the Son of God?! That's a very expensive price to pay for you and me! And God wants us to value ourselves according to His estimate of our worth. God loves us and wants us, or He would not have gone to all that trouble.

But perhaps you say, "Not me; I'm too bad! My character is too scratched and muddy, I'm …." Yes, you and I may have problems, and *be* problems, at times; but listen to this.
- *I Timothy 1:15— "This is a faithful saying, and worthy of all acceptation, that Christ Jesus came into the world to save _____; of whom I am chief."*

Christ came to save us sinners. He died for us while we were still His enemies. That's way beyond awesome! What a hero!

- *Romans 5:7–10— "For scarcely for a righteous man will one die: yet peradventure for a good man some would even dare to die. But God commendeth His love toward us, in that, while we were yet _____, Christ died for us. … For if, when we were _____, we were reconciled to God by the death of His Son, much more, being reconciled, we shall be saved by His life."*

Can anything ever separate us from such a love?

- *Romans 8:35–39—* *"Who shall _____ us from the _____ of Christ? shall tribulation, or distress, or persecution, or famine, or nakedness, or peril, or sword? … _____, in all these things we are more than conquers through Him that loved us. For I am persuaded, that neither death, nor life, nor angels, nor principalities, nor powers, nor things present, nor things to come, nor height, nor depth, nor any other creature, shall be able to separate us from the love of God, which is in Christ Jesus our Lord."*

This amazing God wants us to be with Him for eternity. It will be a place of joy, wholesome pleasures, and NO sickness, suffering, sorrow, or death. Can we *ever* fully understand that love? *(see Psalm 16:11; Revelation 21:3, 4; Ephesians 3:19)*

The future is more than can be imagined, for those who accept God's love and receive Jesus as their Savior, Lord, and Friend.

- *I Corinthians 2:9—* *"Eye hath not seen, nor ear heard, neither have entered into the heart of man, the things which God hath prepared for them that love Him."*

God is thinking, planning for your eternal good.

- *Jeremiah 29:11—* *"For I know the thoughts that I think toward you, saith the Lord, thoughts of _____ and not of evil, to give you an expected end [a future and a hope]"* *(NKJV)*.

Thank you, Jesus!

> **Be a Sleuth**
>
> How can the reality of God's love impact my thoughts about myself? My thoughts about those I interact with? My thoughts about difficult people? My thoughts about those who don't know God's love?

The Purpose for Living

All of nature has a purpose—from the tiny red blood cell, to the largest elephant; from the smallest drop of water to the largest ocean. But what is the purpose for the existence of you and me? Why are we here on this planet?

The Bible, the Word of God, tells us the original purpose.

In the long ago, a loving God created the first people perfect. They looked similar to God Himself. He was the Heavenly Father; they were His children—His friends to care for the earth.

- *Genesis 1:26— "And God said, Let Us make man [people] in Our _____, after Our _____: and let them have _____ over the fish of the sea, and over the fowl of the air, and over the cattle, and over all the _____, and over every creeping thing that creepeth upon the earth."*

In God's Image. That's quite a privilege, to be made in God's image! We are His sons and daughters, His children, created for fellowship with the Lord of the Universe. *(see Revelation 3:20; 4:11; Isaiah 1:18; Jeremiah 33:3; I John 3:2)*

Truly, God wants us to be His friends. The history of the Bible is filled with the story of how much God loves us and is seeking to draw us to Himself.

- *Jeremiah 31:3—* "The Lord hath appeared of old unto me, saying, Yea, I have loved thee with an _____ love: therefore with _____ have I drawn thee."

The ultimate demonstration of this love is shown in the life and death of Christ for our sins. *(see also John 3:16; Matthew 20:28)*

Dominion over the earth. Dominion, that is quite a privilege too! God's style of dominion isn't just to serve self and get all we can. Its purpose is to serve and care for those under one's authority *(Genesis 2:15; Matthew 20:25–28; John 10:11)*. We are here to take care of the earth, and all living things on it.

* * * * * * *

But sin has entered our world, and disrupted God's original plan. So, God gave His Son, Jesus, to save us—from sin's penalty and power, and ultimately from its presence. Now, God's purpose for us also includes: accepting His salvation into our hearts and lives; following His example; and offering His salvation to others. He wants us to be like Him, to live for Him.

- *Philippians 2:5–7—* "Let this mind be in _____, which was also in Christ _____: Who, being in the form of God, … made Himself of no reputation, and took upon Him the form of a servant, and was made in the likeness of men." (see John 3:16; John 20:21; 13:15)

Jesus wants us to love as He has loved, to serve as He has served, and to do as He has done.

- *John 15:12—* "This is my commandment, That ye _____ one another, as I have loved you."

This loving, giving God of ours, wants us to fully give ourselves to Him. That is part of His plan of salvation.

- *II Corinthians 5:15—* "And that He died for all, that they which live should not henceforth live unto _____, but unto _____ which died for them, and rose again."

In return, we gain something in the process of giving. *(see Luke 6:38; Matthew 25:34–40)*

Here are some of the things that He offers to give us.

- *Psalm 16:11—* "Thou wilt shew me the path of _____: in Thy presence is fullness of _____; at Thy right hand there are

The Purpose for Living | 21

_____*for evermore." (see also Matthew 11:28–30; Ezekiel 36:26, 27; Hebrews 10:16; Ephesians 3:16–19; John 1:12)*

Here is more.

- *John 3:16— "For God so loved the world, that He gave His only begotten Son, that whosoever believeth in Him should not perish, but have _____ life." (see also I John 3:1)*

- *John 14:2, 3— "In My Father's house are many mansions ... I go to prepare a place for _____. And if I go and prepare a place for you, I will come again, and receive you unto myself; that where I am, there ye may be also."*

Our Heavenly Father has done so much for us. He longs for us to love Him back. He longs for us to love one another like He has loved us. God still wants that same friendship with us as in the beginning.

- *Revelation 3:20— "Behold, I stand at the door, and knock: if any man hear My voice, and _____ the door, I will come in to him, and will sup [eat] with him, and he with Me." (see also John 17:24)*

Jesus longs for us to open the door of our heart, and invite Him in to guide us, comfort us, and prepare us for eternal life. Won't you accept His offer now?

What about sharing that offer with others?

- *Mark 16:15— "Go ye into all the world, and preach [tell] the gospel to every creature [person].”*

So, what are we here for?

We are here for so many things—things like fellowship with God, caring service for the earth and its inhabitants, salvation applied to our hearts and lives, and sharing the Good News. What a purpose for living! What a privilege is ours!

Be a Sleuth

There are some interesting texts in the Bible that summarize our duty here. How do they say it? How are they similar? *Micah 6:8; Ecclesiastes 12:13, 14; Matthew 22:37–40; Deuteronomy 10:12, 13*

What other texts can you find that talk about our purpose?

Can God be Trusted?

How much can we trust God? How reliable is He?

The natural world and outer space tell us some things about God. The broad sky and the millions of stars tell us that God's power is endless, His majesty is awesome. The flowers and plants tell us that He pays attention to the smallest detail and makes everything perfectly. The birds and animals tell us that He provides for all His creatures. The seasons tell us that God has an appointed time for everything.

The Bible tells us about God's character, as shown in how He deals with humanity. From the days of Creation down to the present time, it tells of His wisdom, love, and mercy. It also shows us His insight, and fairness in dealing with sin and rebellion. God has allowed the principles of evil to work themselves out so that everyone can understand that evil is evil, and good is good. He wants us to understand the broad principles on which He operates, and to trust Him.

Because He loved us so much, God sent His Son, the Creator of the universe, to suffer and die, to save us from sin and its consequences. He willingly did this, so that we rebels might be saved from our self-made destruction. What incomprehensible love! The Creator gave Himself—for you, for me. *(see John 3:16)*

> *The Bible tells us about God's character, as shown in how He deals with humanity. From the days of Creation down to the present time, it tells of His wisdom, love, and mercy.*

What an amazing God! We can trust His wisdom Who made us. We can trust His love Who died for us. We can trust our lives to His care, our hearts to His keeping. We can trust Him in the clean, tidy times. We can trust Him in the sticky, messy times. He's reliable.

Look what He says to us.

- *Matthew 28:20—* "I am with you _____."

That is pretty nice for a Gentleman that's busy running a universe to say something like that!

He's paying attention, too.

- *Matthew 10:30—* "The very _____ of your head are all _____."

He's paying attention all right!

We can open our hearts to Him. "Keep your wants, your joys, your sorrows, your cares, and your fears before God. You cannot burden Him; you cannot weary Him. He who numbers the hairs of your head is not indifferent to the wants of His children" (Ellen White, *Steps to Christ,* p. 100).

He would like us to know His thoughts, and what He's promised to do for us, His children, in every situation of life.

- *Romans 8:28—* "We know that _____ things work together for _____ to them that love God."

God is working in everything for our good. That is more than paying attention; it's being actively involved. What a God! *(see also Deuteronomy 6:24; Psalm 23; I Corinthians 10:13)*

Even when everything seems to be going wrong, we can still trust Him.

- *Habakkuk 3:17, 18—* "_____ the fig tree shall _____ blossom, _____ shall fruit be in the vines, the labor of the olive shall _____, and the fields shall yield _____ meat; the flock shall be cut _____ from the fold, and there shall be _____ heard in the stalls: yet I will _____ in the Lord, I will _____ in the God of my salvation."

We can trust ourselves to His care. When we trust, He will give us peace.

- *Isaiah 26:3, 4—* "Thou wilt keep him in perfect _____, whose mind is _____ on Thee: because he _____ in Thee. Trust ye in the Lord for ever: for in the Lord Jehovah is everlasting strength." *(see also II Corinthians 9:8; John 16:33; Romans 8:32; II Timothy 1:12)*

So when I am having a hard day, and nothing is turning out like I planned, I can still trust God. I can trust that He knows all about it and won't mind me telling Him everything. I can trust that He's working out good, anyway. He will bring me through it all victoriously, as I cooperate with Him. Thank you, Heavenly Father.

Trusting God isn't a one-time-fits-all experience. We must trust day-by-day, moment-by-moment. We must choose to trust God in the good times, in the bad times, and especially when we don't feel like it.

Here's what to do.

- *Psalm 37:5—* "_____ thy way unto the Lord; _____ also in Him; and _____ shall bring it to pass."

Commit thy way unto the Lord—Yes, all your thoughts, your words, your actions, your life, and all your concerns.

Trust also in Him—He's reliable.

He shall bring it to pass—He's an all-powerful partner!

Perfect! He'll get us through those inner struggles, and life's other difficulties.

Over on the other side, we will understand how God truly does all things well. We'll be glad we trusted.

> **Be a Sleuth**
> Trusting God brings peace of mind. What else helps give peace of mind? A clear conscience? A humble heart? Selfless service to others? The death of Mr. Selfishness, Mr. My Way, and Miss Me First? A new life in Christ? Anything more?

Why is There Evil and Misery?

If God is so wise and good, why is there so much suffering and pain in this world? Why am I struggling so? Why is there so much evil and heartache? Why doesn't God just fix everything? Why, Why, Why???

Under the rule of One who is as wise and good as God, there is no excuse for sin and misery. Yet, we can understand enough, about where sin started and its final end, to know that God has dealt with evil wisely and justly.

It is an ancient story. It begins with a wise and loving God, and the beautiful, intelligent beings, called angels, which He created *(see Colossians 1:16, 17; Job 38:4–7)*. They lived in a beautiful, faraway country called Heaven.

Everything was going along fine until the chief angel, Lucifer, got puffed up about his looks and abilities. Instead of being content with his opportunities for service, he wanted to be like God Himself! He wanted to take over.

- *Isaiah 14:12–14— "How art thou fallen from heaven, O Lucifer, son of the morning! … For thou hast said in thine heart, ____ will ascend into heaven, ____ will exalt my throne above the stars of God: ____ will sit also upon the mount of the congregation, in the sides of the north: ____ will ascend above the heights of the clouds; ____ will be like the most High." (see also Ezekiel 28:12–17)*

He had an "I" problem! This self-centered way was totally opposite to the loving, unselfish ways of God and His universe. But God, in His wisdom, didn't just zap him out of existence. He has allowed time for this talented angel to fully show his real character, and to show how his ideas work out. His own work must condemn him.

All the angels, and we humans too, have an opportunity to observe God's plan, and Lucifer's (the devil's) plan. We get to choose which way we want to go.

- *Joshua 24:15— "And if it seem evil unto you to serve the Lord, _____ you this day whom ye will serve." (see also I Kings 18:21; Deuteronomy 30:19; Matthew 4:8–11; Romans 6:16–18)*

In the process of time, Lucifer, now called the devil and Satan, was kicked out of Heaven to this earth. *(see Revelation 12:7–9; Luke 10:18)*

Because of our first parents' (Adam and Eve) fall into sin, the devil now claims dominion over this world. *(see Genesis 3; Matthew 4:8, 9)*

This is why we have such a miserable time of things sometimes.

- *I Peter 5:8— "Be sober, be vigilant; because your adversary the devil, as a roaring _____, walketh about, seeking whom he may _____."*

Yet, in mercy to us, God sets limits on what Satan can and cannot do. *(see Job 1:12)*

But because we live on this earth, we find ourselves in a battle against someone who is stronger than we are.

- *Ephesians 6:12— "For we wrestle not against _____ and _____, but against principalities, against powers, against the rulers of the _____ of this world, against spiritual wickedness in high places."*

The devil does all sorts of evil work. **(1)** He deceives, and persecutes—*Revelation 12:9, 13;* **(2)** He falsely accuses, murders and lies—*Revelation 12:10; John 8:44;* **(3)** He imprisons—*Revelation 2:10;* **(4)** He causes sickness and pain—*Job 2:7;* **(5)** He works signs (miracles)—*Revelation 16:14.*

So, is there hope? Yes! Jesus is our Strong Helper. Look at what He has done for us.

- *Hebrews 2:14, 15— "Forasmuch then as the children are partakers of flesh and blood, He [Christ] also Himself likewise took part of the same; that through death He might _____ him that had the power of death, that is, the devil; and*

_____ them who through fear of death were all their lifetime subject to bondage."

- I John 3:8— *"For this purpose the Son of God was manifested, that He might _____ the works of the devil."*

God is not indifferent to our suffering. Jesus himself came personally to our hurting world and endured much suffering—for our sakes. He feels our pain; He gave His life to relieve it. *(see John 3:16; Hebrews 2:9–11; 4:14–16; Isaiah 53:3–12)*

In the end, God will destroy Satan and sin *(see Ezekiel 28:18, 19; Malachi 4:1)*. Satan is a defeated foe. Christ has conquered on our behalf. Christ is our defense *(Psalm 7:10; 18:17)*.

He offers to us His victory.
- James 4:7— " _____ yourselves therefore to God. _____ the devil, and he will flee from you."

> *God is not indifferent to our suffering. Jesus himself came personally to our hurting world and endured much suffering—for our sakes.*

First submit, then resist.

God is caring for you, and still working out good, despite the evil. *(see Romans 8:28)*
- Psalm 60:12— *"Through God we shall do _____: for He it is that shall tread down our enemies."* (see also Deuteronomy 20:3, 4; Jude 24; I John 4:4; I Corinthians 10:13; Psalm 34:19; I Peter 5:8–11; Isaiah 41:10, 13; 43:1, 2; Revelation 12:11)

Eventually Satan, sin, and sinners (all evil) will be destroyed—they will be burned up. *(see Malachi 4:1; II Peter 3:7, 10, 11)*

Then God will remake this earth new for His followers. *(see II Peter 3:13; Isaiah 65:17; Revelation 21:1–4)*

Sin won't ever come back again! *(see Nahum 1:9)*

Alleluia! Thank you, Jesus!

Be a Sleuth

Where in our lives are we giving our enemy, the devil, an advantage? Isn't it time we removed it?

Power To Choose

The power of choice and freedom of choice are God's gifts to us. God is not going to force us to believe in Jesus. He lets us choose what we will have faith in, what we will believe. That's a generous sovereign to give such dangerous options. It could give Him much happiness, or bring Him a lot of trouble! Still, this absolutely good, thoroughly wise Monarch allows us to choose the good or the bad, the innocent or the evil, life or death.

Even so, God presents to us the better way. He has given us terrific opportunities, at amazing personal sacrifice to Himself! He has given great motivation and incentive, and even offered enabling power for us to do the right. He's done everything that could possibly be done. What a great God! What a kind King!

- *John 3:16, 17— "For God so loved the world, that He gave His only begotten Son, that whosoever believeth in Him should not perish, but have everlasting life. For God sent not His Son into the world to condemn the world; but that the world through Him might be saved."*

God loved. He gave. Whoever chooses belief (faith/trust) in Him, won't perish, but receive eternal life. It's all provided through what Jesus has done for us. What sacrifice! What options!

Although He provides plenty of encouragement to choose the best, God still lets *us* choose.

- *Joshua 24:15—* "_____ you this day whom ye will serve."

- *Deuteronomy 30:19— "I have set before you life and death, blessing and cursing: therefore _____ life, that both thou and thy seed [children] may live."*

Will we choose to serve God, or to follow our own sinful desires? This is what choosing really involves. There are really only two sides to choose from. It is yielding either to God or to Satan, to good or to evil, in every situation of life.

- *Romans 6:16— "Know ye not, that to whom ye _____ yourselves servants to obey, his servants ye are to whom ye _____; whether of sin unto death, or of obedience unto righteousness."*

Jesus understood this. While here on earth, He yielded His personal desires to His heavenly Father's will and ways.

- *Luke 22:42— "Father, if thou be willing, remove this cup from Me: nevertheless not _____ will, but _____, be done."*

We must follow this example, of how Jesus related to every situation of life. We must search out and choose God's way, every time—in the smallest and in the greatest tests.

- *I John 2:6— "He that saith he _____ in Him [Jesus] ought himself also so to _____, even as He walked."*

- *John 14:15— "If ye love Me, _____ My commandments." (see also James 2:17; Galatians 5:6; John 14:21)*

This constant choosing God's way is walking by faith with Jesus. It is allowing Jesus, through the Holy Spirit, to live His obedient life in you and me. *(see Galatians 2:20)*

"Then how important it is that we daily educate and train the will power to render obedience to God in the least as well as in the greatest tests" (*Signs of the Times,* May 15, 1893).

Jesus had the same path to travel as we do. Under difficult circumstances, He too was tempted to disobey God, just as we are. But what did He choose?

- *John 6:38*— *"For I came down from heaven, not to do Mine own will, but the _____ of Him that sent Me."*

By faith in our Heavenly Father, Christ chose to follow God's way, not His own. By faith in God's promises, we can train our minds to *steadfastly* choose God's way instead of our own. This co-operating with Heaven brings victory over temptation. That's good news!

- *I Corinthians 15:57*— *"But thanks be to God, which giveth us the _____ through our Lord Jesus Christ." (see also Revelation 3:21; Luke 22:42; Hebrews 5:8, 9; 12:1–3; II Peter 1:2–4)*

Yet, it is a daily battle. The devil won't let us choose Jesus, without giving us a difficult time. We must, moment-by-moment, maintain a connection with Heaven, and yield our choice to God's way, instead of our way.

- *Luke 9:23*— *"And He said to them all, If any man will come after Me, let him _____ himself, and take up his cross _____, and follow Me." (see also Galatians 2:20; I John 2:15–17; 5:12)*

What has God prepared for those that believe in Jesus, yield to Jesus, and choose to obey Jesus?

- *I Corinthians 2:9*— *"Eye hath not seen, nor ear heard, neither have entered into the heart of man, the things which God hath _____ for them that love Him."*

- *Revelation 22:14*— *"Blessed are they that do His commandments, that they may have right to the tree of life, and may _____ in through the gates into the city."*

Won't you choose Jesus now?
Keep on choosing Jesus.

Be a Sleuth

How can daily scripture memorization help us keep choosing Jesus? How about morning and evening Bible study? How about frequent prayer to God about all the happenings and details of your day?

Faith at Work

Do you ever find yourself doing what you don't allow, and not doing the good that you want to do? Do you ever feel like you're controlled by your sinful habits, and cannot get yourself out of the pit you're in? Take courage; don't despair!

Through Jesus, God offers everyone not only forgiveness, but also healing for the heart and mind, and deliverance from the control of sin. A compassionate Savior, a never-failing Helper, is our Jesus.

- *Matthew 1:21— "He shall save His people _____ their sins."*

No matter how helpless we are to conquer ourselves, in Christ, victory is possible. *(see Romans 6:5, 6; I Corinthians 15:57; II Corinthians 2:14)*

Here's how it works.

- *Ephesians 2:8–10— "For by grace are ye saved through _____; and that not of yourselves: it is the _____ of God: not of works, lest any man should boast. For we are His workmanship, created in Christ Jesus unto good _____, which God hath before ordained that we should walk in them." (see also Romans 8:3, 4; Ephesians 2:20)*

This grace and faith are God's gifts to us, to accomplish in us *"good works,"* since we cannot save ourselves. God planned and provided for this ahead of time.

God has given to everyone, at the least, a scoop of both grace and faith.

- *Romans 12:3— "God has dealt to _____ man the measure [scoop] of _____." (see also Ephesians 4:7)*

Faith is what we use to take hold of God's plan for saving us. Grace is His power to save us. As we cooperate with Jesus' work of saving us, we will receive more scoops of grace and faith. *(see Ephesians 3:16–19)*

What this gift of faith is, and how faith works, can be understood in a story. God had promised Abraham and Sarah that they would have a baby. Years had gone by, and now Sarah was passed the time of life when she could have children. It seemed impossible that the promise could come true. Yet, what does the Bible tell us about Abraham's faith?

- *Romans 4:20, 21— "He staggered _____ at the promise of God through unbelief; but was strong in faith, giving glory to God; and being _____ _____ that, what He [God] had promised, He was able also to perform."*

Abraham believed, even in the face of seeming impossibility. His belief was more than just mental acceptance of a fact. He trusted God fully. *(see Genesis 26:5; Hebrews 11:8–10; II Timothy 1:12)*

Abraham's kind of faith is what we need. It was made for action.

Faith is awake and doing something. We can tell it is there by what it is doing.

- *James 2:17— "Faith, if it hath not _____, is dead."*

- *John 1:12— "But as many as _____ Him, to them gave He power to become the sons of God, even to them that _____ [that's faith] on His name." (see also I Peter 2:24; consider also the "by faith" and "through faith" statements in Hebrews 11)*

Notice the action in the following statement:

"Where there is not only a belief in God's word, but a submission of the will to Him; where the heart is yielded to Him, the affections fixed upon Him, there is faith—faith that works by love and purifies the soul. Through this faith the heart is renewed in the image of God" (Ellen White, *Steps to Christ, p. 63).*

That is a kind of faith worth having.
Is this faith only active at the beginning of our Christian journey?
- *I John 5:4*— *"This is the _____ that overcometh the world, even our _____."*

If we want to continue to overcome the world, we must continue to have faith in Jesus—not in things or people.

Faith is an essential part of victorious Christian living all along the way. Through grace and faith, our lives are changed.
- *John 8:31, 32*— *"If ye _____ in My word, then are ye My disciples indeed; and ye shall know the truth, and the truth shall make you _____." (see also I John 2:5)*

This means, that in every situation we face, we must exercise our faith and accept God's grace. We do this by choosing Christ and His way, as found in the Bible, instead of our own way. *(see John 6:38)*

Even though I can't conquer myself by myself, look at what is possible through ongoing faith in Jesus.
- *Mark 9:23*— *"Jesus said unto him, If thou canst believe, _____ are possible to him that believeth."* *(see also Philippians 2:13; II Peter 1:2–5; II Corinthians 2:14; Philippians 4:19)*

> *Faith is an essential part of victorious Christian living all along the way. Through grace and faith, our lives are changed.*

What God asks us to do, His grace enables us to do through faith. Through faith at work, a life of victory is possible. The plan of salvation includes so much! Thank you, Jesus.

Keep choosing Christ. Keep faith at work.

Be a Sleuth

How does trusting, obedient faith claim God's promises? What would a prayer of faith be like? Shouldn't I try such a prayer now?

Where in my daily life should I put faith to work first? And next? And next?

The Gift of Grace

"God is able to make all grace abound toward you; that ye, always having all sufficiency in all things, may abound to every good work"
(II Corinthians 9:8).

God likes giving gifts. Step out into nature and you will see many skillfully made, beautiful gifts. At the fruit market, the eyes and tongue can appreciate the colorful, delicious gifts.

In nature, God's lovely gifts can be felt, His peace experienced. In the spiritual realm, there are even greater gifts.

Salvation is the free gift of being saved from sin *(Matthew 1:21; John 3:16)*. The gift of grace, through the gift of faith in Jesus, is how it happens. These gifts make possible our receiving of the gift of eternal life. What a gift-giving God!

Let's look more at this gift of grace. What is it?

- *Ephesians 2:8—* "For by grace are ye _____ through faith; and that not of yourselves: it is the gift of God." (see also John 3:16, 17; Galatians 3:26; Romans 5:21)

- *Romans 1:16—* "For I am not ashamed of the gospel of Christ: for it is the _____ of God unto salvation to every one that believeth; to the Jew first, and also to the Greek."

Grace is God's forgiving, transforming power, to save everyone who believes in Christ. It has been planned for us, since before the world began—before there was a need. *(see Jeremiah 31:3; II Timothy 1:9; Titus 2:11–13)*

It is sin that has made the need for God's grace. We cannot save ourselves from the natural consequences of sin, which is death. We need a Savior.

- *Romans 3:23, 24— "For _____ have sinned, and come short of the glory of God; being justified [forgiven] _____ by His _____ through the redemption that is in Christ Jesus." (see also Acts 4:12; Romans 5:20, 21; 6:23; Proverbs 28:13; I John 1:9)*

But God's free gift of saving grace is available to all. Through sorrow for sin, confession, and faith in Christ, we may be forgiven, even though we don't deserve it.

But grace doesn't end at forgiveness; it keeps on going. Grace enables obedience. It not only works in our hearts, but also in our lives.

- *Romans 1:5— "By whom [Christ] we have received _____ and apostleship, for _____ to the faith among all nations, for His name."*

- *II Corinthians 9:8— "And God is able to make all _____ abound toward you; that ye, always having all sufficiency in all things, may abound to _____ good work."*

Grace keeps going beyond forgiveness, beyond obedience. Grace enables us to rejoice, to be like Jesus, even in uncomfortable situations.

- *II Corinthians 12:9, 10— "And He [God] said unto me, My _____ is _____ [adequate] for thee: for My strength is made perfect in weakness. Most gladly therefore will I rather glory in my infirmities [weaknesses], that the power of Christ [that's grace] may rest upon me. Therefore I take _____ in infirmities, in reproaches, in necessities, in persecutions, in distresses for Christ's sake: for when I am weak, then am I strong."*

Grace for forgiveness. Grace for obedience. Grace for rejoicing to reflect Christ, even in life's difficulties. God's marvelous grace!

This grace is only available to us through Jesus!

- *Romans 5:1, 2— "Therefore being justified by faith, we have peace with God through our Lord _____ _____: by whom also we have access by faith into this grace wherein we stand, and rejoice in hope of the glory of God."*

God's grace works through His Word to build us up.
- *Acts 20:32— "And now, brethren, I commend you to God, and to the _____ of His grace, which is able to _____ you up, and to give you an inheritance among all them which are sanctified."*

The promises of the word of grace will make us more like Jesus, *if* we allow our lives to continue to be shaped by them, inside and out.
- *II Peter 1:2–4— "Grace and peace be multiplied unto you through the knowledge of God, and of Jesus our Lord, according as His divine power hath given unto us all things that pertain unto life and godliness, through the knowledge of Him that hath called us to glory and virtue: whereby are given unto us exceeding great and precious _____: that by these ye might be partakers of the divine nature, having escaped the corruption that is in the world through lust." (see also Romans 11:22)*

All the power of Heaven is ready to help us in our need. God wants to give us a glorious inheritance.

Through daily Bible study, continued faith, and obedience to God's word, His grace can be ever increasing in our lives. Through God's grace we may take part in the divine nature and escape the corruption in this world. *(see Ephesians 2:8; Hebrews 7:25)*

What marvelous grace!

Be a Sleuth

Practically, how do we continue our daily, moment-by-moment connection with Christ and His grace? *(See John 8:31, 32; John 15:9–11; I John 2:24, 25)*

Take Your Conscience to School

Where have you taken your conscience to school? Yes, I'm sure your mom and dad have done their best to help educate your conscience properly. But, where have YOU been educating you conscience lately? The TV? Your friends? Your music? Your job? Your perceptions and opinions? What you read? God's word? How will your conscience tell you what is right and wrong if you haven't sent it to the right school?

What is our conscience for anyway? Well, you know, really it is that part of your thinking that tells you that you're not being a good boy or a good girl, a good man or a good woman. It's that helpful part of you that says, "You'd better not do that; it's not right."

And of course, it is best to listen to our conscience. We wouldn't want it condemning us, would we? That was always the apostle Paul's policy.

- *Acts 24:16— "And herein do I _____ [exert] myself, to have always a conscience void [empty] of offence [wrong doing] toward God, and toward men."*

Paul made sure he gave his conscience no reason to condemn him. He wanted to make sure everything was right between himself and God, and between himself and those around him. *(see Acts 23:1)*

Take Your Conscience to School | 39

That's a good way to live. But of course, it takes a certain willingness on our part.

- *Hebrews 13:18—* "*Pray for us: for we trust we have a _____ conscience, in _____ things willing to live _____.*"

We must be willing to live honestly in order to have a good conscience.

Also, we must take an honest look at our lives, and make them match up with the Word of God. We really must live like the Bible tells us we should, in order to have a pure, clean conscience.

- *I Corinthians 10:31—* "*Whether therefore ye eat, or drink, or _____ ye do, do _____ to the glory of God.*" *(see also Colossians 3:17; Romans 12:1, 2)*

That is the way to have an accurate, properly functioning conscience. If we measure what is right or wrong by some other standard, our conscience won't guide us properly. We must not think how the neighbors do it, or what can get us the most advantage, or any other consideration. We can't even trust our emotions. Our feelings are unreliable.

- *Jeremiah 17:9—* "*The heart is _____ above all things, and desperately wicked: who can know it?*"

We must:

- *II Timothy 2:15—* "*_____ to shew thyself approved unto God, a workman that needeth not to be ashamed, rightly dividing the word of truth.*" *(see also II Timothy 3:16, 17)*

And

- *II Corinthians 13:5—* "*_____yourselves, whether ye be in the faith; prove your own selves.*"

We must examine our own hearts and lives by the Word of God.

What can happen to the conscience if we don't keep on sending it to the school of God's Word? It can be come dirty, defiled, bent, or burnt.

- *I Timothy 4:1, 2—* "*Now the Spirit speaketh expressly, that in the latter times some shall _____ from the faith, giving heed to seducing spirits, and doctrines of devils; speaking lies in hypocrisy; having their conscience _____ [burnt] with a hot iron.*" *(see also Titus 1:15; Isaiah 5:20–24)*

We don't want that happening to us.

So, of course, you'll keep sending your conscience to the school of God's Word, right?! For truly, you will continually need Teacher Jesus' help, and the Holy Spirit's reminders, to keep the conscience as it should be.

- *Hebrews 9:14— "How much more shall the blood of Christ, who through the eternal Spirit offered Himself without spot to God, purge [thoroughly clean] your _____ from dead works to serve the living God?" (see also I Timothy 1:5)*

Serving God with a good, pure conscience is the best way to live. You'll be glad you did. (So will those who have to live with you.) ☺

Be a Sleuth

What are the benefits of a well-educated conscience? To keep it clean and good, what should you avoid?

Guilty

Guilty, hmmm. Worthless, condemned, a failure ... Ohhh! That sounds pretty miserable! How do we get out of this uncomfortable situation?

Well, actually, *some* guilt is beneficial. It helps stop us from a path of evil and turns our thoughts and actions to what is right and good.

But, we can also have a misguided sense of guilt, condemnation, worthlessness, or sense of failure. We can feel bad or guilty for owning useful shoes when others have none, or for eating strawberries on Friday, or for taking a nap when we need one, or for doing less than a very precise job, or for being a few pounds more than skin and bones.

Guilty or not—how can we really tell? How do we deal with the guilty feeling that we have now?

To begin with, we are all guilty of sin—breaking God's law.

- *Romans 3:23— "For all have _____, and come short of the glory of God." (see also Romans 5:12; I John 3:4)*

We all deserve sin's penalty, yet we also have access to its solution.

- *Romans 6:23— "For the wages of sin is _____; but the gift of God is eternal _____ through Jesus Christ our Lord."*

Our acceptance of Jesus' life, death, and resurrection, on our behalf, erases our guilt. Christ took our guilt upon Himself that we may go free.

- *John 3:16—* *"For God so loved the world, that He gave His only begotten Son, that _____ believeth in Him should not perish, but have everlasting life." (see also II Corinthians 5:21; I Corinthians 15:2; I Peter 2:24; 3:18)*

So then, a sense of guilt for our wrongdoing sends us to Christ for relief and forgiveness. In this way, a sense of guilt can work for our eternal good. It is part of the helpful work done for us by the Bible and the Holy Spirit. *(see Proverbs 6:23; John 16:7–14)*

So, how do we personally receive Christ's gift of freedom from the guilt of sin?

- *Proverbs 28:13—* *"He that covereth his sins shall not prosper: but whoso _____ and _____ them shall have mercy."*

- *I John 1:9—* *"If we _____ our sins, He is faithful and just to forgive us our sins, and to cleanse us from all unrighteousness."*

"If you give yourself to Him, *[Christ]* and accept Him as your Saviour, then, sinful as your life may have been, for His sake you are accounted righteous. Christ's character stands in place of your character, and you are accepted before God just as if you had not sinned" (Ellen White, *Steps to Christ, p. 62)*.

You are freed from guilt. That is wonderful!!!

But even after this we may still feel guilty at times. Sometimes it is because the Holy Spirit is revealing something "new" to us that needs changing to be more like Jesus. None of us is perfect yet, you know.

- *John 16:8—* *"And when He [the Holy Spirit] is come, He will _____ the world of sin, and of righteousness, and of judgment." (see also v. 13)*

God wants to do more than just forgive our sins and remove our guilt; He wants to give us each a new heart and mind. He wants to empower us for holy living.

- *Ezekiel 36:26, 27—* *"A _____ heart also will I give you, and a _____ spirit will I put within you: and I will take away the stony heart out of your flesh, and I will give you an heart of flesh. And I will put my spirit within you, and cause you to* walk in my statutes, and ye shall _____ my judgments, and do them."

- II Corinthians 5:17— "Therefore if any man be in Christ, he is a _____ creature: old things are passed away; behold, all things are become new."

We must, in faith, connect with Christ in the work of character development.

- II Corinthians 7:1— "Having therefore these promises, dearly beloved, let us cleanse ourselves from all filthiness of the flesh and spirit, perfecting _____ in the fear of God."

Keep searching the scriptures as a guide for every area of your life. It contains life principles for those that keep on prayerfully looking.

- II Timothy 3:16, 17— "All scripture is given by inspiration of God, and is profitable for doctrine, for reproof, for correction, for instruction in righteousness: that the man of God may be perfect, thoroughly furnished unto all good works."

There is a lying devil out there who wants to keep you in bondage to fear, needless guilt, anger, and other negative patterns of thoughts and living. He wants to keep you from living to your full potential.

But how do you go about changing? The same way that you confessed and abandoned your sins, when you first believed in and received Christ. This is how to continue the rest of your Christian life.

- Colossians 2:6, 7— "As ye have therefore _____ Christ Jesus the Lord, so _____ ye in Him: rooted and built up in Him, and stablished in the faith, as ye have been taught, abounding therein with thanksgiving." (see also John 8:31, 32; I John 2:5, 6; I Peter 1:15)

What about when that old, worthless, I'm no good, I'm guilty feeling comes back? Even after you've confessed your negative habits, and abandoned them—even when you're not guilty? Or perhaps you feel guilty for doing something wholesome and good.

There is a lying devil out there who wants to keep you in bondage to fear, needless guilt, anger, and other negative patterns of thoughts and living. He wants to keep you from living to your full potential. He wants you to lose your faith in Christ and give up.

- *Luke 22:31, 32*— *"And the Lord said, Simon, Simon, [and you too,] behold, Satan hath desired to have you, that he may sift you as wheat: but I have prayed for thee, that thy _____ fail not: and when thou are converted, strengthen thy brethren." (see also I Timothy 4:1; I John 4:1)*

Christ is your hope; don't give up! You are *very precious* to Him. And remember to return to the Bible to understand whether those worthless, no-good, guilty feelings are from God or not. Examine your life and what you are thinking, according to the Word of God. *(see II Timothy 2:15; II Corinthians 13:5)*

If you continue in God's Word with a willingness to surrender and change what He reveals to you, you can walk with a clean conscience—forgiven and freed! Jesus died to set you free. Won't you accept Him and His offer, now?

Here is a promise for those who follow Jesus.

- *John 8:31, 32*— *"If ye continue in My word, then are ye My disciples indeed; and ye shall know the truth, and the truth shall make you _____."*

You can be free from guilt, both real and imagined!

Be a Sleuth

How does comparing ourselves to those around us give us a false sense of worth or worthlessness, condemnation, or a sense of guilt? *(see II Corinthians 10:12)*

My Way

We all have life patterns and habits of response that are comfortable or familiar to us—the way we brush our teeth; how we deal with time; how we tie our shoes; and how we speak to our brother, or the pet kitten, or the lady on the phone, or the pushy salesman ….

Perhaps we've grown up with flawed habits of perception or response, or developed them since then. We are so used to them, that we have a hard time even fully recognizing how bad we are. Our sinful natures want to justify our selfish, un-Christlike behaviors and twisted thinking patterns.

- *Proverbs 21:2— "Every way of a man is right in his _____ eyes: but the Lord pondereth the hearts." (see also Luke 16:15)*

It all originates in the thoughts of our hearts *(see Matthew 12:34; Proverbs 23:7)*. We all have done wrong, and justify our own ways of thinking and behaving. *(see Proverbs 16:2)*

Christ came to pay the penalty for our wrongs.

- *Isaiah 53:6— "_____ we like sheep have gone astray; we have turned every one to his _____ way; and the Lord hath laid on Him the iniquity of us all."*

But is there anything wrong with seeing our ways—habits—as being right?

- *Proverbs 16:25—* "*There is a way that seemeth _____ unto a man, but the end thereof are the ways of _____.*"

Our own natural, self-centered ways of thinking lead to death, rather than life. Sin has affected even *our* ways of thinking. Our natural ways are out of harmony with God's ways. The natural result of following our own ways is physical illness and mental and spiritual struggles.

God's Word, the Bible, is the only true guide for how we should behave.

- *Psalm 119:105—* "*Thy word is a lamp unto my feet, and a _____ unto my path.*" *(see also Psalm 16:11; 17:4, 5; II Timothy 3:16, 17)*

Sinful humanity doesn't know how to behave properly.

- *Jeremiah 10:23—* "*O Lord, I know that the _____ of man is not in himself: it is _____ in man that walketh to direct his steps.*"

Why?

- *Jeremiah 17:9—* "*The heart is _____ above all things, and desperately _____: who can know it?*"

For a list of the things that the natural, sinful heart produces, *see Galatians 5:19–21; Romans 1:28–32; Matthew 15:19, 20.*

Try as we might, we can't fix our own hearts. We can't save ourselves. *(see Ephesians 2:8–10)*

How then can we be free from the power of these natural, sinful habits of our flesh?

- *Romans 8:1–6—* "*There is therefore now no condemnation to them which are _____ Christ Jesus, who walk not after the flesh [natural sinful desires], but after the _____. For the law of the Spirit of life in Christ Jesus hath made me _____ from the law of sin and death. ... For they that are after the flesh do mind the things of the flesh; but they that are after the Spirit the things of the Spirit. For to be carnally minded is death; but to be spiritually minded is life and peace.*" *(read the whole passage—Romans 8:1–12; also Ezekiel 36:26, 27)*

Thank God for making a way of escape for each of us through the Holy Spirit working in our hearts and minds. It is left to us to yield to God and ask Him to give us new hearts.

Then, since God never forces anyone, we must co-operate with His work in our hearts. We must think His thoughts. *(see Romans 12:1, 2; Philippians 4:8)*

God will work with and in us to replace the evil with the good.

- *II Corinthians 2:14— "Now thanks be unto God, which always causeth us to _____ in Christ, and maketh manifest the savour of His knowledge by us in every place."*

- *I Corinthians 15:57— "But thanks be to God, which giveth us the _____ through our Lord Jesus Christ." (see also Philippians 2:12, 13; Ephesians 4:22–32; Colossians 3:2, 8–10)*

What a privilege is ours to have the transforming help of Heaven! Through Christ, a better way (than our own way) is available for our lives.

Be a Sleuth

Can I mentally know God's word without being transformed by it? How does yielding to Christ and receiving His power work out practically in my life?

The Power of the Plan

There is a powerful plan provided by the King of the universe. It is the plan of salvation. What is it all about?

It's an old story, of a loving God and the people that He created. When they disobeyed His reasonable rules *(sin, see I John 3:4)*, the Son of God Himself offered to pay the penalty of transgression *(disobedience)*. He became a human, lived on this earth, and died to save us from our sins.

- *Titus 2:13, 14— "Looking for that blessed hope, and the glorious appearing of the great God and our Saviour Jesus Christ; Who gave _____ for us, that He might redeem us from _____ iniquity, and purify unto Himself a peculiar people, zealous of good works." (see also Matthew 1:21; John 3:16; Romans 6:23; I Peter 1:18–20)*

The Son of God, Jesus, took our death penalty, that we might go free.

- *I Peter 2:24— "Who His own self bare our sins in His own body on the tree, that we, being dead to sins, should live unto righteousness: by whose stripes ye were healed."*

"Christ was treated as we deserve, that we might be treated as He deserves. He was condemned for our sins, in which He had no share, that we might be justified by His righteousness, in which we had no share. He suffered the death which was ours, that we might receive the life which was His. 'With His stripes we are healed'" (Ellen White, *The Desire of Ages,* p. 25).

What an incredible price to pay to rescue rebellious humanity! What amazing love!

It is left to us to decide whether we will accept and cooperate with this offer, or not.

What must we do to be saved from our sins? Penance? Pilgrimages? Thankfully, it is much simpler than that, and it is free.

- *Acts 16:31—* "_____ *on the Lord Jesus Christ, and thou shalt be saved."*

This belief is more than a mental acknowledgment of a fact. This belief receives Christ. This means a faith in Christ that accepts His death on the cross to pay the death penalty I deserve for my sins. This belief also receives Christ into my heart as Lord and Guide of my life.

- *John 1:12—* "*But as many as _____ Him, to them gave He power to become the sons of God, even to them that believe on His name." (see also Revelation 3:20)*

That emptiness we feel, that no amount of possessions, people, or places can fill, is a symptom of our inner need of the living Christ. Only Jesus can satisfy that inner thirst.

- *John 4:14—* "*But whosoever drinketh of the water that I shall give him shall never _____ ; but the water that I shall give him shall be in him a well of water springing up into everlasting life." (see also Matthew 5:6; Psalm 23:2)*

There are two things that we must receive when we believe *(have faith)* in Christ—His death and His life.

- *Romans 5:10—* "*For if, when we were enemies, we were reconciled [reconnected] to God by the _____ of His Son, much more, being reconciled, we shall be saved by His _____ ."*

Accepting Christ's death for me brings me forgiveness. Accepting His life into my life brings the healing of salvation. It is Christ's victory working out practically in my life. *(see Romans 8:1–4; II Corinthians 2:14; 5:17; John 8:31, 32, 36; Colossians 1:27)*

With my consent, Jesus wants to live His life of victory in me! He wants to free me from the cruel bondage of sinful habits.

- *Galatians 2:20*— *"I am crucified with Christ: nevertheless I live; yet not I, but Christ _____ in me: and the life which I now live in the flesh I live by the faith of the Son of God, who loved me, and gave Himself for me."*

The life of faith is a life of action. Through a living, moment-by-moment connection, Christ empowers His followers to live His way—to follow His example and to obey His word. Our life will give evidence of our connection with Christ and His Word.

- *I John 2:5, 6*— *"Whoso keepeth His _____, in him verily is the love of God perfected: hereby know we that we are in Him. He that saith he abideth in Him ought himself also so to _____, even as He walked." (see also James 1:22–25; 2:17, 20)*

For those who continue in Christ and obey His Word, there is a promise.

- *John 8:31, 32*— *"If ye _____ in My word, then are ye My disciples indeed; and ye shall know the truth, and the truth shall make you _____."*

There is also the promise, to believers, of an eternal life of happiness in a wonderful place—heaven.

- *John 14:1–3*— *"Let not your heart be troubled: ye believe in God, believe also in Me. In my Father's house are many mansions: if it were not so, I would have told you. I go to prepare a place for you. And if I go and prepare a place for you, I will come again, and receive you unto Myself; that where I am, there ye may be also." (see also John 3:16)*

- *Psalm 16:11*— *"Thou wilt shew me the path of life: in Thy presence is fulness of joy; at Thy right hand there are pleasures for _____."*

Please also read *Revelation 21:1–5*.

I want to be there; how about you?! Why not decide now? Invite Jesus to live in your heart, and to guide your life. You will be glad that you did.

Be a Sleuth

What are the current benefits of yielding yourself and your life to Christ?

He Didn't Treat Me Nicely!

Don't we wish everyone treated each other nicely?! Don't we wish *we* were always treated nicely? But since that won't happen, and since even God Himself doesn't get treated nicely; what are we to do?

First of all, what has God done with His problem people? What does His Word tell *us* to do?

God has many angel helpers in heaven with Him. But long ago, the brightest one rebelled against God's rulership. By telling lies, he got many of the angels to also rebel. Now he is called the devil or Satan. What did God do (after much patience and effort) to win him back?

- *Revelation 12:7, 9— "And there was _____ in heaven. … And the great dragon was _____ _____, that old serpent, called the Devil, and Satan, which _____ the whole world: he was cast out into the earth, and his angels were cast out with him." (see also Isaiah 14:12–17; Ezekiel 28:11–19)*

That's pretty drastic! But sometimes those kinds of things need to be done. Sometimes we need to get rid of a bad situation or remove ourselves from it. But, the Bible has some very interesting principles for dealing with difficult people, and even our enemies.

We all know the story of the human race rebelling against God, of a whole race choosing disobedience and death rather than life and truth.

We know the story of the Creator giving all, even His life, to save us from our self-made destruction, to show us His awesome love, and to win our hearts.

- *Romans 5:8, 10—* "*God commendeth [demonstrates] His love toward us, in that, while we were yet _____, Christ died for us. ... For if, when we were enemies, we were reconciled to God by the death of His Son, much more, being reconciled, we shall be _____ by His life.*"
- *Luke 19:10* "*The Son of Man [Jesus] is come to _____ and to _____ that which was lost.*"

God's motives for treating those that wrong Him are much, much better than getting even, or giving them what they deserve. He doesn't even cut off His love from them. God has no self-centered, self-pleasing, or selfish motives. He thinks only for the best good of His universe.

Here on this planet, it is His studied purpose to win each person from the power of darkness, and to transform them into His kingdom of light. *(see Acts 26:18)*

Yet, it is true that not everyone will respond positively to God's efforts to win and transform their hearts. In the end, those opposed to God, who persistently go away from Him, will be left to their own course. Yes, in the end *God*, not us, will destroy sin, and whoever clings to it. But let us follow His saving plan for how we should treat difficult people.

> *Here on this planet, it is His studied purpose to win each person from the power of darkness, and to transform them into His kingdom of light.*

Considering how God has dealt with disagreeable people, how does He want *us* to deal with them?

- *Ephesians 4:32—* "*Be ye _____ one to another, _____, _____ one another, even as God for Christ's sake hath forgiven you.*"

Do you need help forgiving? Ask God; He'd be glad to help. *(see Hebrews 4:14–16; Ephesians 2:8–10)*

What's next?

- *Proverbs 25:21, 22—* *"If thine _____ be hungry, give him bread to eat; and if he be thirsty, give him water to drink: for thou shalt heap coals of fire upon his head, and the Lord shall reward thee."*

- *Matthew 5:44, 45—* *"_____ your enemies, _____ them that curse you, do _____ to them that hate you, and _____ for them which despitefully use you, and persecute you; that ye may be the children of your Father which is in heaven: for He maketh His sun to rise on the evil and on the good, and sendeth rain on the just and on the unjust."*

- *Romans 12:18—* *"If it be possible, as much as lieth in you, live _____ with all men."*

We are responsible for our own attitudes and responses.

What God asks us to do, He will help us do. His grace is big enough to take care of our needs. *(see II Corinthians 12:9)*

As we keep seeking Jesus—the healing salve—our wounds will heal. *(see Jeremiah 8:22; Luke 4:18; Ezekiel 34:15, 16)*

Be a Sleuth

What must we do to make sure that we don't show un-Christlike behaviors? Can Jesus give us what is necessary on the inside, to be nice on the outside? *(see Ephesians 3:16–20)*

Forgive? But She ...!

What she did was bad. What she said was worse. Quickly, all sorts of thoughts and feelings start bubbling up inside. Uh oh!

What are we to do? Getting even isn't a worthwhile option, neither is giving them what they deserve *(see Romans 12:17, 19; Proverbs 24:29).* A flood of angry words isn't God's way, neither is a truckload of unkind responses. What are we to do? *(see Proverbs 21:23; Ephesians 4:32; James 1:19, 20)*

Jesus, the Man of Peace, has showed us the way, and He can also calm the storm within.

What is His example? Has anybody wronged God?
- Romans 3:23— "For _____ have sinned, and come short of the glory of God." *(see also I John 1:8)*

That means everybody has wronged God and treated Him terribly. I don't suppose it feels nice to Him, either. I'm sure His heart is wounded. So what has He done about it? He's invented a way to fix the problem, and win us back, if we are willing. It is called forgiveness. *(see Psalm 86:5; Romans 3:23, 24; I John 1:9; Proverbs 28:13)*

God paid quite a high personal cost—the life of His Son, Jesus—in order to forgive us.

- *John 3:16— "For God so _____ the world, that He _____ His only begotten Son, that whosoever believeth in Him should not perish, but have everlasting life."*

And notice the purpose of God's forgiveness. It is to reclaim, if possible, the one who has done wrong, who has wounded Him.
- *John 3:17— "For God sent not His Son into the world to condemn the world; but that the world through Him might be _____."*

That is quite an example for us to contemplate. But *us* forgive??? Ouch! That's not comfortable to our natural hearts! Yet it is true, that the physical and emotional effects of keeping our wounds fresh in our minds is much *more uncomfortable* to ourselves and to those around us. Certainly, we must learn from our wounds. But, the only way for our wounds to heal is to forgive. Christ has forgiven you; He will help you to forgive those who have wounded you.

It is a privilege to join in that forgiveness which seeks, where possible, to safely reclaim. Forgiving, transforming, and reclaiming go together in God's plan. His forgiveness toward us is more than a legal transaction. Its purpose is to transform our thinking and doing. In order for that to happen, we must forgive those who have wounded us. We must forgive like we have been forgiven.
- *Ephesians 4:32— "And be ye kind one to another, tenderhearted, _____ one another, even as God for Christ's sake hath forgiven you."*

This privilege of forgiving others is actually a condition for us to be forgiven by God.
- *Matthew 6:14, 15— "For if ye _____ men their trespasses, your heavenly Father will also forgive you: but if ye forgive _____ men their trespasses, neither will your Father forgive your trespasses."*

This is reasonable. If we truly value how God has forgiven us, we will want to pass it on.

God has not left uncertain what forgiveness is like. It's a choice … well, many choices. In this verse His perfect example shows us what to do.
- *Micah 7:18, 19— "Who is a God like unto thee, that _____ iniquity, and passeth by the transgression of the remnant of His heritage? He _____ _____*

His anger for ever, because He _____ in mercy. He will turn again, He will have _____ upon us; He will _____ our iniquities; and Thou wilt cast all their sins into the _____ of the sea."

Pardoneth iniquity—God forgives. It's a choice.

Passeth by the transgression—God chooses not to think about it. He doesn't bring it up. *(Isaiah 43:25; Hebrews 10:16, 17)*

He retaineth not His anger—He doesn't hold on to anger.

He delighteth in mercy—Instead, He delights in mercy.

He will have compassion—That starts with filling the thoughts with good things. *(Philippians 4:8; Luke 10:30–37; Jeremiah 29:11)*

He will subdue our iniquities—Beyond mercy, beyond compassion, He works to benefit us. Yes, God is forever working to reclaim us. *(Romans 12:20, 21)*

Into the depths of the sea—God wants to thoroughly cleanse our hearts, if we will give Him permission—and let go.

I need to forgive more deeply; what about you?

Certainly, we may have to remind ourselves again and again of these principles. We must also keep returning to God for more of His transforming grace for our hearts. But, the more we take God's principles into our lives, the more we will become like Jesus. We must keep at it.

Even though forgiving is essential, there are situations where it is not safe to renew contact with those who have harmed us. Some problems cannot be fully repaired. Remember this verse.

- *Romans 12:18*— *"If it be _____, as much as lieth in you, live _____ with all men."*

Yet, we can let the peace of God rule in our hearts, by forgiving. And by and by, our feelings will catch up with the choices that we have made—and keep making.

Be a Sleuth

How can I best apply these principles to my current situation, and yet keep myself safe?

Problems—Why?
Part 1

Have you ever thought that troubles could be God's workmen to bring benefit to your life? It's God's refining fire, purifying our character—to be like glistening gold.

Problems ... we all have them, right?! They disturb our sense of wellbeing, don't they? (to put it mildly!) And we all want to get rid of them, don't we? That would be more comfortable. But that's not possible in this sinful old world.

Have you ever thought that troubles could be God's workmen to bring benefit to your life? It's God's refining fire, purifying our character—to be like glistening gold.

- Isaiah 48:10— "Behold, I have refined thee, but not with silver; I have chosen thee in the furnace of _____ [difficult times]."

- *I Peter 1:7*— "That the trial of your faith, being much more _____ than of gold that perisheth, though it be tried with fire, might be found unto praise and honour and glory at the appearing of Jesus Christ."

No matter where life's troubles come from—our fault, someone else's fault, or the devil's fault—God wants to use them for our good. Even if we feel frightened, frustrated, angry, distressed, or overwhelmed, God is working for our good. Even when we are tempted to think, speak, or act like our enemy, the devil, instead of like Jesus, our best Friend, God is still working to bring about good.

Being tempted to think or act like the devil isn't sin, but yielding is. Just remember that God has an amazing plan for you. His plan is to transform life's troubles into His workmen, to perfect *(transform)* your character—to be like Jesus. Look at what is possible, even in life's difficulties, with God's help!

- *II Corinthians 4:8–10*— "We are troubled on every side, yet not _____; we are perplexed, but not in _____; persecuted, but not _____; cast down, but not _____; always bearing about in the body the dying of the Lord Jesus, that the _____ also of Jesus might be made manifest in our body."

Wow! Through Jesus' death for us, life's problems can be turned for our benefit. We may have Jesus' victory and peace in our lives, in our daily difficulties, as well as in those significant situations. *(please read II Corinthians 4:15–18; Romans 5:3–5; 8:28)*

It's like exercise! We get more benefit exercising on a hill than on level ground, right? But in life's problems, we need not face the hill alone. Christ has done the hill—the hill of Calvary—before us. He offers to go with us and give us His strength.

- *II Corinthians 12:9, 10*— "And He said unto me, My _____ is sufficient for thee: for My strength is made perfect in weakness. Most gladly therefore will I rather glory in my infirmities, that the _____ of Christ may rest upon me. Therefore I take _____ in infirmities, in reproaches, in necessities, in persecutions, in distresses for Christ's sake: for when I am weak, then am I strong." (see also James 1:2–4; Hebrews 4:15, 16)

Those verses actually say that we are to take pleasure in life's difficulties, so we may receive power from God! Wow! That's radical thinking! But there are great opportunities and privileges in such thinking and living. Yet we must be willing, and cooperative, if we are to gain the benefit. *(see Romans 8:17, 18; I Peter 5:10)*

To bring good out of life's troubles, God uses the Holy Spirit, working through His Word, the Bible *(see John 16:13–15)*. We should ask God to enlighten our minds, by the Holy Spirit, as we read the Word. We will receive help and instruction for life's difficulties.

- *Psalm 107:20— "He sent His _____, and healed them, and delivered them from their destructions."*

- *Psalm 17:4— "Concerning the works of men, by the _____ of Thy lips I have kept me from the paths of the destroyer." (see also Hebrew 4:12; II Peter 1:2–4; John 16:13–15)*

Certainly, what God asks us to do, He provides the means to get the job done. *(see II Corinthians 12:9; I Corinthians 10:13; I Thessalonians 5:24; II Thessalonians 3:3)*

We have hope. We know that our loving God rules over all. He has our best good in mind.

- *Jeremiah 29:11— "For I know the thoughts that I think toward you, saith the Lord, thoughts of _____, and not of evil, to give you an expected end."*

He is limiting the power of evil, and working out *all* things for our good.

- *John 19:11— "Jesus answered, Thou couldest have _____ power at all against Me, except it were given thee from above."*

- *Romans 8:28— "And we know that _____ things work together for _____ to them that love God, to them who are the called according to His purpose."*

He will give us what we spiritually need to make it through to the other side successfully.

- *I Corinthians 10:13— "There hath _____ temptation taken you but such as is common to man: but God is _____, who will not suffer you to be tempted _____ that ye are able; but will with the temptation also make a way to escape, that ye may be able to _____ it."*

We may not understand *why* God has allowed some of the difficult parts of our lives *(see John 13:7)*, but we can know that our loving Heavenly Father *is* bringing good out of everything. When He makes all things new, He will wipe away all tears from our eyes and hearts. *(see Revelation 21:1–4)*

> ## Be a Sleuth
> Does Jesus care? Where is He when life is difficult? *(Read Hebrews 13:5; Isaiah 49:15, 16; 41:13; 42:16; and Psalm 23)*

Problems—Why?
Part 2

In part one, we discussed how God wants to bring us through each problem in life, hopeful and victorious. He is working out our eternal good, even in life's difficult times. God transforms life's troubles unto His workmen to perfect our characters. The Holy Spirit, through the Bible, brings God's grace and power to us. If we co-operate with Him, He will give us what we need to make it to the other side successfully.

- *Isaiah 41:13— "For I the Lord thy God will hold thy right hand, saying unto thee, Fear not; I will _____ thee." (see also Romans 8:28; I Corinthians 10:13)*

The Bible tells us some of the reasons why we have problems. Not every reason applies to each situation. In fact, we may not have all our *why* questions answered until we get to heaven and can ask Jesus Himself. I am sure He will be glad to explain everything then *(see John 13:7; I Corinthians 4:5)*. Until then, let's trust Him to take care of our why questions.

Why? A few reasons…
Here are some of the reasons why troubles come to us.

1) To show us the problems in our own hearts. Then we can co-operate with God in replacing those defects with Christ-like habits.

- *Deuteronomy 8:2— "And thou shalt remember all the way which the Lord thy God led thee these forty years in the wilderness, to _____ thee, and to _____ thee, to _____ what was in thine heart, whether thou wouldest keep His commandments, or no." (see also Proverbs 16:25; Jeremiah 10:23; 17:9)*

- *Psalm 119:75— "I know, O Lord, that Thy judgments are right, and that Thou in _____ hast afflicted me." v. 71 "It is good for me that I have been afflicted; that I might _____ Thy statutes." v. 67 "Before I was afflicted I went astray: but now have I kept Thy word." (see also Deuteronomy 8:3, 16; I Peter 5:10, 11)*

Some lessons can only be learned under difficult circumstances.

When Christ shows us the problems in our hearts, then He can lead us in a better way.

- *Psalm 139:23, 24— "Search me, O God, and know my _____: try me, and know my _____: and see if there be any wicked way in me, and _____ me in the way everlasting." (see also Jeremiah 29:11; John 19:11; Romans 8:28; I Corinthians 10:13)*

2) Our troubles help us to help others better. We can empathize, and share, with them what has helped us.

- *II Corinthians 1:3, 4— "Blessed be God, even the Father of our Lord Jesus Christ, the Father of mercies, and the God of all comfort; Who comforteth us in all our tribulation [troubles], that we may be able to _____ them which are in any trouble, by the comfort wherewith we ourselves are comforted of God."*

Been there, done that.

Even if we have to endure trouble because of someone else's bad choices, we can still gain wisdom and strength from the experience. This can benefit not only ourselves, but also others. *(see Proverbs 24:30–32; Hebrews 5:8, 9)*

3) That Christ's life may be revealed in us.
- *II Corinthians 4:8–10—* *"We are troubled on every side, yet not distressed; we are perplexed, but not in despair; persecuted, but not forsaken; cast down, but not destroyed; always bearing about in the body the dying of the Lord Jesus, that the _____ also of _____ might be made manifest in _____ body."*

As Christ died for us, we must die to our own sinful ways, so Christ's life may be revealed in us. We can't produce enough goodness on our own. We need the life of Christ, like a spring of water, bubbling up in our hearts. *(see John 4:14)*

Anyone can look friendly and helpful when things are going their way. But true Christianity shines brightest in the darkness of inconvenience, interruptions, irritations, and more serious difficulties. Facing problems Christ's way reveals the life of Jesus. It is a privilege to reveal the living Christ to those who don't know Him.

- *II Corinthians 3:2, 3—* *"Ye are our epistle written in our hearts, _____ and _____ of all men: forasmuch as ye are manifestly declared to be the epistle of Christ ministered by us, written not with ink, but with the Spirit of the living God; not in tables of stone, but in fleshy tables of the heart."*

And we can face problems with joy, knowing they are making us more like Jesus.

- *James 1:2–4—* *"My brethren, count it all _____ when ye fall into divers temptations; knowing this, that the trying of your faith worketh _____. But let patience have her perfect work, that ye may be perfect and entire, wanting nothing."*

- *II Corinthians 4:17, 18—* *"For our light affliction, which is but for a moment, worketh for us a far more _____ and _____ weight of glory; while we look not at the things which are seen, but at the things which are not seen: for the things which are seen are temporal; but the things which are not seen are eternal." (see also Romans 5:1–5)*

We must focus our attention not so much on how troubling the problem is, but rather on the unseen spiritual benefits. When we keep everything in perspective, then we can see the joy.

So what now?

Because life's problems aren't easy or comfortable, we need more than a knowledge of *why* to get us through them triumphantly. In brief, here is what to do.

A) Connect with Heaven—the power source of the universe.
- *I Thessalonians 5:17— "Pray without _____."* (see also II Corinthians 9:8)

B) Yield to God.
- *James 4:7, 8— "_____ yourselves therefore to God. Resist the devil, and he will flee from you. Draw nigh to God, and he will draw nigh to you."*

C) Determine to do things God's way.
- *Romans 12:21— "Be not overcome of evil, but overcome evil with _____."* (see also Joshua 1:7–9; John 8:31, 32)
- *I Corinthians 10:31— "Whether therefore ye eat, or drink, or whatsoever ye do, do _____ to the glory of God."*

D) In everything give thanks—especially because of God's promises.
- *I Thessalonians 5:18— "In _____ thing give thanks: for this is the will of God in Christ Jesus concerning you."*
- *Romans 8:28— "And we know that _____ things work together for good to them that love God, to them who are the called according to His purpose."*

The Sympathizing Savior is our helper. He has endured life's difficulties. He understands. He is ready to help. What a wonderful Jesus!!!

Be a Sleuth

What other workmen does God use to make us more like Jesus? Do we have to co-operate, in order to gain a benefit?

Responding to Difficulties God's Way
Part 1: The Crisis

Responding to difficulties God's way, that sounds great! Really, it does! It *is* great. But we don't always find it easy. Why? Well, we really know, don't we? Life's difficulties are, well, difficult, or uncomfortable, or otherwise unpleasant. Our selfish natures don't like being uncomfortable, or disturbed, or slighted, or insulted, or ….

We can find help in the powerful promises of God's Word. Even if we are weak and failing, we need not despair. We must look to the word of God and the sympathizing Savior Who stands ready to help us.

- *Isaiah 41:13— "For I the Lord _____ God will hold thy right hand, saying unto thee, _____ _____; I will _____ thee."*

He has promised. Trust Him. Choose His way. He *will* help you.
OK, so when some difficulty comes along, what am I to do?

STOP and pray.

At the very beginning of life's difficulties and temptations, STOP, and instantly send up a prayer to God.

- *Romans 12:12—"Rejoicing in hope; patient in tribulation; continuing _____ in prayer."*
- *Psalm 55:22— "_____ thy burden upon the Lord, and He shall sustain thee: He shall never suffer the righteous to be moved."*

Refuse to act on any thought or feeling that is not in harmony with God's will. *(James 1:22; Jude 24; II Corinthians 10:4, 5)*

Ask God to protect you from evil (inside and out) and to give you strength to be faithful. Even if you're uncertain why you are feeling like you're feeling, take it to the Lord.
- *Psalm 138:3— "In the day when I cried [prayed] Thou answeredst me, and _____ me with strength in my soul."*

Mix thanksgiving with your prayers.
- *Philippians 4:6, 7— "Be careful [anxious] for _____; but in every thing by prayer and supplication with _____ let your requests be made known unto God. And the peace of God, which passeth all understanding, shall keep your hearts and minds through Christ Jesus." (see also Psalm 50:15; I Thessalonians 5:18)*

Notice the *"with thanksgiving"* part. Adding thanksgiving to our calls for help, helps to transform the difficult situation into a victorious one. Try something like this: "Help me, Lord! I feel _____! I choose to respond to this Your way. Thank You, for promising to strengthen me to be faithful to You *(Psalm 138:3)*. Thank You for Your promise to supply all my needs *(Philippians 4:19)*. Thank You for causing me to triumph *(II Corinthians 2:14)*. In Jesus' dear name, amen."

If you must respond promptly, do your best to respond as you believe Jesus would respond in this situation.

If your response may wait, search God's Word for what to do, then respond. *(see Psalm 27:14; 40:1, 2; James 1:5, 6; Isaiah 41:13)*

Examine your thoughts.
Is what I am thinking *now*, in harmony with God's Word? Just because you are thinking or feeling something doesn't make it true. Look in the Bible.

Responding to Difficulties God's Way | 67

- *Psalm 139:23, 24— "Search me, O God, and know my heart: try me, and know my _____: and see if there be any wicked way in me, and _____ me in the way everlasting."*
- *II Corinthians 13:5— "_____ _____, whether ye be in the faith; prove your own selves."*

> *Is what I am thinking now, in harmony with God's Word? Just because you are thinking or feeling something doesn't make it true.*

We cannot change the past, but we must examine our own thoughts and feelings in the light of God's Word, and take responsibility for our own actions. We can choose to respond differently today.

Feelings or emotions are produced by our thoughts. They are an unreliable guide to discern God's will for our lives. We must not base our decisions on emotions or related physical symptoms. We must compare our thinking and feeling to the Word of God. We must settle in our hearts to do things God's way. *(see Proverbs 3:5, 6; I Corinthians 10:31; Daniel 1:8)*

Here is what to do next.

Search the Word.

- *Psalm 119:105— "Thy word is a _____ unto my feet, and a _____ unto my path." (see also II Timothy 3:15–17; John 5:39)*

Find scripture commands and promises that apply to your difficulties and to your temptations to display negative responses.

Memorize the Word.

- *Psalm 119:11— "Thy word have I _____ in mine _____, that I might not sin against thee."*

Use the Word.
- *Psalm 17:4*— "Concerning the works of men, by the _____ of Thy lips I have kept me from the paths of the destroyer [the devil]."

Here's how.
- *Romans 12:21*— "Be not overcome of evil, but _____ evil with good."

When we face life's difficulties and temptations, we must replace our negative, unhealthy, sinful, or evil thoughts with the good Word of God. We must overcome evil with good.

Quote the Word.
Quote the Word to yourself and to the enemy.
- *Matthew 4:3, 4*— "And when the tempter came to Him, he said, If Thou be the Son of God, command that these stones be made bread. But He [Jesus] answered and said, _____ _____ _____, Man shall not live by bread alone, but by every word that proceedeth out of the mouth of God."

Keep connected to the Word.
We must stay in connection to the Author of the Word.

Talk to God. Perhaps you're staring at fear. Talk with God, saying something like this:

"Kind Father, help me. You know what I'm feeling. Thank you for promising in Isaiah 41:13 'For I the Lord thy God will hold thy right hand, saying unto thee, Fear not; I will help thee.' Thank you, that You are trustworthy. Thank you, that You are faithful. Thank you, that You will bring me through this situation, *more* than a conqueror. Thank you, for caring for me. In Jesus' precious name, amen."
- *Isaiah 26:3*— "Thou wilt keep him in perfect peace, whose mind is _____ on Thee: because he _____ in Thee."

Despite circumstances or emotions, keep thinking about the written Word. Keep talking to the Living Word—Christ Jesus. Keep following Jesus through what He has given us in the Bible. *(see I John 2:5, 6)*

There is power—life—in Christ, the Word.

- *John 1:4—* "*In Him [Jesus] was life, and the life was the light of men.*" *(see also John 14:6)*

Connect, reconnect, keep connected.

OK, here is the summary.

STOP. Pray with thanksgiving. Examine your thoughts. Search the Word. Memorize the Word. Use the Word. Quote the Word. Keep connected to the Living Word.

Be a Sleuth

Why is the Word of God so important when dealing with life's difficulties? (*II Timothy 3:15; Hebrews 4:12; I Peter 1:22, 23; Psalm 119:98, 99*)

Responding to Difficulties God's Way
Part 2: The Long Term

In part *one* we studied about what to do when life's difficulties come along. The first step was to STOP. The next step was to pray to God with thanksgiving for His promises. After that we should examine our thoughts. Then we need to search the Word, memorize the Word, use the Word, and quote the Word. Through it all we must stay connected to the Living Word, Christ Jesus.

Now we will study additional things that help us face life's difficulties victoriously.

Look to Jesus.

When confronted with temptation, don't look to circumstances or your own weakness; look to Christ Jesus!

- *Hebrews 12:1, 2— "Wherefore seeing we also are compassed about with so great a cloud of witnesses, let us lay aside every weight, and the sin which doth so easily beset us, and let us run with patience the race that is set before us, _____ unto _____ the Author and Finisher of our faith; Who for the joy that was set before Him endured the cross, despising the shame, and is set down at the right hand of the throne of God."*

Serve others.
Helping others helps yourself.
- *Galatians 6:2— "Bear ye one _____ burdens, and so fulfil the law of Christ." (see also Proverbs 11:25; Luke 6:38)*

Give thanks.
Despite the past, despite the present, despite the prospects for the future, give thanks to God. Give thanks—for Who God is, for what He has done, for His specific promises about the present and the future.
- *I Thessalonians 5:18— "In every thing give _____: for this is the will of God in Christ Jesus concerning you." (see also I Corinthians 15:57)*

Study the Bible and pray daily.
Daily Bible study and prayer is essential in victorious Christian living.
- *II Timothy 2:15— "_____ to shew thyself approved unto God, a workman that needeth not to be ashamed, rightly dividing the word of truth."*

- *John 15:4, 5— "Abide in Me, and I in you. As the branch _____ bear fruit of itself, except it abide in the vine; no more can ye, except ye abide in Me. I am the vine, ye are the branches: He that _____ in Me, and I in him, the same bringeth forth much fruit: for without Me ye can do nothing."*

Live healthfully.
Healthful living helps us be victorious in our mental and spiritual struggles.

- *III John 2—"Beloved, I wish above all things that thou mayest prosper and be in _____, even as thy soul prospereth."*

Focus on the good.
- *Philippians 4:8—"Finally, brethren, _____ things are true, whatsoever things are honest, whatsoever things are just, whatsoever things are pure, whatsoever things are lovely, whatsoever things are of good report; if there be any virtue, and if there be any praise, _____ on _____ things."*

Don't invite temptation.
When we are trying to get rid a bad personal habit, we need to get rid of things associated with that bad habit, and avoid the situations that entice us back into the bad habit. We need the power of Jesus and the help of all Heaven in this work. Then it will be truly successful and heart changing.
- *Romans 13:14—"But put ye on the Lord Jesus Christ, and make _____ _____ for the flesh, to fulfil the lusts thereof." (see also Colossians 3:1–3)*

Do something better.
Plan something worthwhile in place of the bad habit.
- *Romans 12:21—"Be not overcome of evil, but overcome evil with _____."*

Trust and obey.
Remember, don't yield to your emotions, but trust God to guide you and take care of you. Determine to obey Him.
- *Proverbs 3:5, 6—"_____ in the Lord with all thine heart; and lean not unto thine own understanding. In _____ thy ways acknowledge Him, and He shall direct thy paths."*

Responding to Difficulties God's Way | 73

- *I John 2:6—* "He that saith he abideth in Him ought himself also so to walk, even as He walked." (see also I Corinthians 10:31)

Keep at it.

Continuing in God's way brings freedom from the old harmful habits.
- *John 8:31, 32—* "Then said Jesus to those Jews which believed on Him, If ye _____ in My _____, then are ye My disciples indeed; and ye shall know the truth, and the truth shall make you _____."

If you lose a battle, don't give up the war against the old ways.
- *Romans 8:37—* "Nay, in _____ these things we are more than _____ through Him that loved us." !!!

Continued co-operation with Christ creates conquerors.
If you fall, take hold of Christ again, and He will help you up.
- *Psalm 37:23, 24—* "The steps of a good man are ordered by the Lord: and he delighteth in His way. Though he fall, he shall not be _____ cast down: for the Lord upholdeth him with His hand."

- *Micah 7:8—* "Rejoice not against me, O mine enemy: when I fall, I shall _____; when I sit in darkness, the Lord shall be a light unto me." (see also v. 9; Proverbs 24:16; Jude 24)

Dear friends, let's face it. Sometimes the struggle with life's difficulties and our own sinful nature gets long and fierce. The Bible has some timely advice for us – take heart, look up.
- *Joshua 1:9—* "Have not I commanded thee? Be strong and of a good _____; be not afraid, neither be thou dismayed: for the Lord thy God is with thee whithersoever thou goest."

- *Galatians 6:9—* "And let us not be _____ in well doing: for in _____ _____ [at the right time] we shall reap [harvest], if we faint not."

- *Hebrews 12:2–4—* "_____ unto _____ the Author and Finisher of our faith; Who for the joy that was set before Him endured the cross, despising the shame, *and is set down at the right hand of the throne of God. For _____ Him that endured such contradiction of sinners against Himself, lest ye be wearied and faint in your minds. Ye have not yet resisted unto blood, striving against sin." (see also John 14:23; 17:3; II Corinthians 5:14, 15; Galatians 5:6; I John 2:5, 6)*

Take courage. Look to Jesus. He will help you.

> **Be a Sleuth**
>
> What lifestyle choices help us to keep the victory?
>
> What are some wholesome ways to help us get our minds off our troubles? Helping others worse off than ourselves? Doing something creative? Learning something new? Exercise in the fresh air? Time in the garden, park, or woods?

To Be Like Jesus

"Now unto Him that is able to keep you from falling, and to present you faultless before the presence of His glory with exceeding joy" (Jude 24).

Have you ever wanted to be more like Jesus? He was so kind and patient, loving and loyal, courageous and wise, and just plain good. Of course you have! Jesus is wonderful!

Jesus Himself wants you to be like Him. He wants the very best for you and me. The Bible shows us this better way.

Yet sometimes we choose the way of disobedience. But disobedience is more than just disobedience; it is a cruel master that can hold even *you* in bondage *(see John 8:34; Romans 6:16)*. But even now, there can be victory by faith in Christ.

Through a combination of the grace of God, our faith in Christ, and the empowering of the Holy Spirit, a victorious life is possible. What a way to live! *(see Matthew 1:21; Acts 3:26; II Corinthians 7:1)*

We were originally made in God's image, but because of sin, we have all fallen short of God's original design *(see Genesis 1:27; Romans 3:23)*. Yet God has a plan of restoration and hope in the gospel. He is working out His plan, even amid difficult situations.

- *Romans 8:28— "And we know that _____ things work together for _____ to them that love God, to them who are the called according to His purpose."*

God's plan is that we become like Jesus.
- *Romans 8:29— "For whom He did foreknow, He also did predestinate to be conformed to the _____ of His Son, that He might be the firstborn among many brethren." (see also Jeremiah 29:11; I John 3:2, 3)*

God's plan of restoration in our lives has three parts: **(1)** Justification—a legal transaction of forgiving. Because of Christ's death on the cross for us, when we repent, confess our sins, and yield ourselves to God, we are justified—forgiven *(see Romans 5:1; I John 1:9)*. **(2)** Sanctification—becoming more like Jesus. This is a life-long process. It involves a daily, continued growing faith in God. Daily we must co-operate with Christ, choose His good ways, and let Him live in us *(see II Thessalonians 2:13, 14; Colossians 2:6, 7)*. **(3)** Glorification—the change to immortality at Jesus' second coming. *(Romans 8:16–18; I Corinthians 15:53, 54)*
- *Hebrews 7:25— "Wherefore He [Christ] is able also to save them to the _____ that come unto God by Him, seeing He _____ liveth to make intercession for them."*

This lesson will be focusing on sanctification, and our co-operation with Christ's work of restoring us ***to be like Jesus.***

Sanctification leads to holiness. This is God's plan for us.
- *I Peter 1:15, 16— "But as He which hath called you is holy, so be ye _____ in all manner of conversation; because it is written, Be ye holy; for I am holy."*

Sanctification is the process of co-operating with God's work of purifying our lives and making us holy—wholly like Him. Thus we receive His traits of character.

Sanctification, holiness, becoming like Jesus, is very important. Look at this text.
- *Hebrews 12:14— "Follow peace with all men, and _____, without which _____ man shall see the Lord."*

Spending eternity in Heaven with God depends on our joining in God's work of sanctification in our everyday lives. To be more like Jesus in our thinking, our words, our actions, our responses, must be our constant aim.

We are called to faithfully pursue holiness—that holiness found in Jesus. We want to continue to have more of His ways as our ways, and His life in our life. *(see Jeremiah 6:16; I John 2:6; Proverbs 4:18)*

So how do we go about changing?

God uses the truths of His Word to sanctify us—to help us become like Jesus.

- *John 17:17— "Sanctify them through Thy _____: Thy _____ is truth."*

We are sanctified by obeying the truth, through the power of the Holy Spirit. *(see I Peter 1:22)*

- *Acts 20:32— "And now, brethren, I commend you to God, and to the _____ of His _____, which is able to build you up, and to give you an inheritance among all them which are _____." (see also II Peter 1:2–4)*

The Bible is the absolute standard of right and wrong, truth and error. If we want holiness in our thoughts and responses to life's situations, we must shape our lives according to the truths of God's Word *(see II Timothy 3:15–17)*. The Word + grace = sanctification. Apply it in every situation of life.

Jesus, our Savior and Helper, is the living Word of God.

- *John 1:14— "And the _____ [Christ] was made flesh, and dwelt among us, (and we beheld His glory, the glory as of the only begotten of the Father,) full of grace and truth."*

The Holy Spirit changes us, as we behold Jesus in His Word.

- *II Corinthians 3:18— "But we all, with open face _____ [looking intently] as in a glass [mirror] the glory of the Lord, are _____ into the same image from glory to glory, even as by the _____ of the Lord." (see also John 14:26)*

Jesus is everything to us! Look to Jesus. Look to His Word.

The more we look to Jesus, the more we put His Word into our hearts, the more we will copy Him, and the more we will be like Him. Isn't that what you want?

- *I John 3:2, 3— "Beloved, now are we the sons of God, and it doth not yet appear what we shall be: but we know that, when He shall appear, we shall be _____ Him; for we shall see Him as He is. And every man that hath this hope in him _____ himself, even as He is pure."*

Of course, all the power of heaven backs up the Bible. Sanctification is a work of co-operation. We can't purify ourselves without Jesus' help. He won't purify us without our co-operation.

- *II Corinthians 7:1— "Having therefore these promises, dearly beloved, let us _____ ourselves from all filthiness of the flesh and spirit, _____ _____ in the fear of God."* (see also I Thessalonians 5:23, 24; I Peter 1:22; Philippians 2:12, 13)

We are not in this process alone! Therefore, we must keep connecting with Jesus in order to be successful. *(see John 15:5)*

Through His life and death, Christ has provided everything you need, so that you may partake in His holiness. He will be with you all the way.

- *Titus 2:14— "Who gave _____ for us, that He might redeem us from all iniquity, and purify unto Himself a peculiar people, zealous of good works."*

Keep working side-by-side with Jesus. He is faithful, and He will help you to be faithful, also. *(see Philippians 1:6)*

> *Through His life and death, Christ has provided everything you need, so that you may partake in His holiness. He will be with you all the way.*

Be a Sleuth

What areas of our lives need to be sanctified? Our behaviors? Our activities? Our thoughts? Our words? Our responses to people? Our choices? How shall we begin?

Looking to Jesus

"Looking unto Jesus the Author and Finisher of our faith; Who for the joy that was set before Him endured the cross, despising the shame, and is set down at the right hand of the throne of God. For consider Him that endured such contradiction of sinners against Himself, lest ye be wearied and faint in your minds" (Hebrews 12:2, 3).

  Here's where to begin the Christian walk. Here's where to go for help when we need it—help for character development, strength for bearing trials, help with our thoughts, our attitudes, our words and actions. Here's where to go when we're weary on the Christian path. Start here, in joy or sadness, health or illness, ease and plenty.

  Look to Jesus when you're tempted or perplexed, when you're suffering or wounded. Look to Jesus when you're battling self or Satan. Look to

Jesus when you need a friend. Look always to Jesus. Not only His teaching, but also His example, is inspiring. Look to Jesus.

Look to Jesus **at the beginning of the Christian walk.** *(Read the Gospels.)*

See **Christ's love for you.** *(John 3:16; Romans 5:7–10; I John 3:1)*

See that **He is a friend of sinners.** *(John 8:3–11; Mark 2:16, 17; Romans 5:8; I Timothy 1:15)*

Look to Jesus when you need **repentance** *(Mark 2:17; Luke 15:11–32; Acts 5:31)*, and **forgiveness** *(Luke 23:33, 34; I John 1:9; Luke 6:37; Luke 7:36–50; Acts 5:31)*.

Look at Christ's example and promises when you are in need of **patience.** *(Psalm 40:1, 2; John 19)*

Look to Jesus for **courage** *(Matthew 10:24–26, 29–32; 28:20; I Thessalonians 5:24; II Corinthians 9:8)*, for **joy** *(Luke 15:3–7; Hebrews 12:2, 3; III John 4; I Peter 1:7, 8; John 15:1–11; Galatians 5:22, 23)*, for **trust** *(Matthew 8:23–27; Luke 12:22–32; Proverbs 3:5, 6; Isaiah 12:2)*.

See how Jesus dealt with **overwhelming emotions ... dread, pain, despair ...** for you, yet didn't give up. *(Matthew 26:36–39)*

Look at **Jesus' peace** during stormy circumstances. How did He do it *(Mark 4:35–41; Luke 20:19–26; John 16:32, 33; 18:1–11)*? He **offers us His peace,** and all the help we need. *(John 14:27; Isaiah 26:3, 4; 27:5; 48:18)*

See **how He treated His enemies.** *(Luke 23:33, 34; Matthew 5:43–48; Romans 12:18–21)*

What was Christ's response to **those who treated Him unkindly and unjustly?** *(Matthew 5:38–41; I Peter 2:20–24; Isaiah 53)*

Look to the cross **when you feel wounded.** *(Hebrews 12:2, 3; Luke 22:54–62; Isaiah 53:4, 5; John 19; I Peter 4:19)*

Look at how gently He dealt with **His betrayer** *(John 13:2–5, 21–30; Luke 22:21, 22)* and **His murderers.** *(Luke 23:33, 34)*

See how Jesus dealt with **the grieving** *(Mark 5:35, 36, 39; Luke 7:11–16; John 11:21–27)* and **the desponding.** *(Luke 7:19–29; John 5:1–9)*

See how sympathetic He was to **the sick.** *(Matthew 8:2–7, 16; 9:2, 22; Luke 6:17–19)*

See how Jesus **encouraged the young** *(Matthew 19:13–15)* **the old** *(Exodus 20:12; Mark 7:9–13; 12:41–44; John 19:25–27; James 1:27; Leviticus 19:32), and* **the weak.** *(John 8:2–11; Isaiah 42:1–3; Mark 14:32–38; Luke 22:31, 32)*

Look how He **walked with the Father** every step of the way. *(John 8:29; 16:32)*

Look to Jesus, Who was **tempted for you.** *(Matthew 4:1–11; Hebrews 4:14–16)*

Look to Jesus as He **chose His Father's way instead of His own.** *(John 6:38; Luke 22:42)*

See how He faced **a difficult future**, when yours seems impossible. *(John 16:32, 33; Luke 22:42, 43; Psalm 119:28; Isaiah 43:1, 2; II Corinthians 4:15–18; Romans 8:18, 28; I Peter 3:13–18; 4:12–19)*

He is a **sympathizing Savior.** Think how He treated human need. *(Psalm 103:13, 14; Hebrews 4:15, 16)*

See how He **treated the poor** *(Mark 12:41–44; 14:7; Luke 4:18)* and **the rich.** *(Matthew 19:16–26; Luke 19:1–10; James 5:1–6)*

See His **humility** when you are tempted with **pride.** *(Philippians 2:5–8; II Corinthians 8:9; Luke 17:10; Matthew 5:3; 20:25–28)*

Look how Jesus dealt with **those slow to learn.** *(John 16:12; Mark 4:33; Luke 24:25–27)*

Look to Jesus as He dealt with **the light and frivolous.** *(John 4:5–30)*

See His response when people **disappointed Him.** *(Luke 22:31–34, 54–62; John 21:15–19; 14:6–14)*

What did He do when people **abandoned Him**? *(Isaiah 42:1–4; Matthew 26:31, 32, 56; John 6:66–69)*

How did Jesus Himself deal with **the limitations of poverty?** *(Luke 22:35; Matthew 6:24–34; 8:20; II Corinthians 8:9)*

How did Jesus treat **the overconfident**? *(Luke 9:51–56; 22:24–27; Matthew 17:14–21; 20:20–28; 26:30–35)*

Look how He dealt with those that **didn't realize their inner need.** *(John 3:1–21; 4:5–26)*

What did Jesus have to say about **forgiving**? *(Matthew 6:14, 15; 18:21–35)*

When you feel **weary on the Christian walk,** look again at what Christ endured for you. *(John 18 and 19)*

Look and see what kind of Man He was. Receive His life as your own, for all that He has, He has given that you may become like Him. *(Romans 8:32; Hebrews 4:14–16; Philippians 2:5–8; II Corinthians 9:8)*

Be a Sleuth

What does the mind tend to focus on, instead of looking to Jesus? Self? Personal problems? People? Money? Things? Entertainment? Sinful pleasures? And …? How am I going to remedy the problem? What will help me keep looking to Jesus?

Anger

Anger? Uh oh!

Have you ever thought that you don't have to let anger into your yard? It may be barking madly at your gate, and jumping at your fence, but you don't have to let it in your yard! But if it's already in your yard, you don't have to feed it, or keep it there. It is a mad dog that will bite you and your family.

There is a story about a young man named Joseph who seemed to have had every right in the world to get angry. His brothers yanked off his fabulous, costly coat, and confiscated it. They insulted him, refused to share their lunch with him, and made him go hungry. Finally, they sold him to be a slave in a foreign land. He had every right in the world to be angry.

In that foreign land, Joseph endured much hardship and even imprisonment because he was determined to do what was right. Through it all he persistently chose to trust God, and live God's way. He maintained a forgiving attitude, refusing to let anger and bitterness run his life.

In God's providence, and because of his sterling character, he was eventually appointed to a position of power and influence.

Years later, when his brothers came to his country, it would have been very easy for him to inflict prompt and bitter revenge, but he didn't.

Instead, he tested their characters, to see if they had changed. They had. Listen to what he said to them.

- *Genesis 45:5— "Now therefore be not grieved, nor angry with yourselves, that ye sold me hither: for God did send me before you to preserve life."*

What a forgiving attitude! What trust in God!

Even after his father's death, when his brothers worried again that he might take revenge, Joseph repeated the same thoughts.

- *Genesis 50:19–21— "And Joseph said unto them, Fear not: for am I in the place of God? But as for you, ye thought evil against me; but God meant it unto good, to bring to pass, as it is this day, to save much people alive. Now therefore fear ye not: I will nourish you, and your little ones. And he comforted them, and spake kindly unto them."*

Joseph refused to keep anger in his heart. He chose a better way. That way is available to you and me. We don't have to hold on to anger. We can let it go. *(see Ephesians 4:31, 32; Psalm 37:8)*

Giving up anger doesn't justify the wrong doer, or his deeds. It doesn't excuse the wrong. It sets you free. *(see John 8:32; II Corinthians 3:17; Luke 4:18; Galatians 5:1)*

Besides, as I tell my children, we are responsible for our responses.

- *Psalm 51:3— "For I acknowledge _____ transgressions: and my sin is ever before me." (see also Psalm 37:8; Ecclesiastes 7:9)*

The event, and your response to it, are two different things. Own up to your actions. Don't blame the situation or other people. Don't justify or deny. Be responsible for your own response. *(see Psalm 32:5; I John 1:9)*

Besides, if we step back a few paces from the situation, and look at things in the light of Calvary, and eternity, anger will usually seem small and petty.

When we become angry, it is often because self doesn't like how life is going, or feels wronged in some way. Self doesn't like to be wounded, slighted, neglected, or taken advantage of. It doesn't like not having its expectations met or not getting its way. And it especially doesn't enjoy doing disagreeable duties. But when we give our hearts and lives to God, we will trust ourselves to His keeping, and not take these things so much to heart.

- *II Timothy 1:12*— *"For I know whom I have believed, and am persuaded that He is able to _____ that which I have committed unto Him against that day." (see also I Peter 2:21–23; 4:19)*

We must put off the old man of sinful self and his ways. We must be dead to the old life, and alive to Christ.
- *Colossians 3:1–3*— *"If ye then be risen with _____, seek those things which are above, where Christ sitteth on the right hand of God. Set your affection on things above, not on things on the earth. For ye are dead, and your life is hid with Christ in God." (see also Colossians 3:9, 10)*

We must put on Christ and His ways.
- *Romans 13:14*— *"But _____ ye _____ the Lord Jesus Christ, and make not provision for the flesh, to fulfil the lusts thereof."*

But to be sure, the old, sinful, selfish man wants to rise from the dead and talk to you. That mad dog will again bark at your gate. Don't listen to it, and don't be anxious about it. There is help from above.
- *Psalm 119:28*— *"My soul melteth for heaviness: _____ Thou me according unto Thy word."*

Since anger, like other wrong actions, grows out of our thinking, it must be dug out by the roots—not just chopped off at the top.
- *Psalm 139:23, 24*— *"Search me, O God, and know my heart: try me, and know my thoughts: and see if there be any wicked way in me, and _____ me in the way everlasting."*

In our mad dog illustration, we must let go of the thought leash. Sometimes anger creeps up on us quickly. Before we know it, he's in our yard, we're holding his leash, and he's biting everyone within reach. But remember, no matter how fast it happens, or how fierce his barking, we are responsible if he's in our yard. Our thoughts, our words, and our actions must be controlled. We are not in this struggle alone. We can connect with God and His grace.
- *II Corinthians 10:4, 5*— *"(For the weapons of our warfare are not carnal, but mighty through God to the pulling down of strong holds;) casting down _____, and every high thing that exalteth itself against the knowledge of God, and bringing*

into captivity every _____ to the obedience of Christ." (see also Romans 12:2)

Christ can help us take that mad dog out of our yard and keep it out. Go to the Word of God when you hear anger barking.

- *Psalm 119:11— "Thy _____ have I hid in mine heart, that I might not sin against Thee."*

Memorize and repeat texts that directly apply to your situation. *(see Romans 12:17-21; Proverbs 21:23; 24:29; 25:28; 15:17; 16:32; Psalm 37:8)*

Remember the following steps (see also "Responding to Difficulties God's Way," parts 1 and 2):

When you hear anger barking, STOP.

Go to God for help. Talk to Him about the situation, and the promises of His word.

- *Romans 12:12— "Rejoicing in hope; patient in tribulation; continuing _____ in prayer."*

- *Psalm 55:22— "_____ thy burden upon the Lord, and He shall _____ thee: He shall never suffer the righteous to be moved."*

Refuse to let your mind travel those negative roads of thinking that lead to anger. Keep your mind focused on God and His word.

- *Isaiah 26:3, 4— "Thou wilt keep him in perfect peace, whose _____ is stayed on Thee: because he _____ in Thee. Trust ye in the Lord for ever: for in the Lord Jehovah is everlasting strength."*

Persevere. Keep at it, no matter how many times the mad dog barks at your gate.

- *John 8:31, 32— "If ye _____ in My word, then are ye My disciples indeed; and ye shall know the truth, and the truth shall make you _____."*

Get a new pet. Leave no room for the mean old dog. Put something better in its place.

- *Romans 12:21— "Be not overcome of evil, but _____ evil with good."*

- *II Corinthians 5:17*— *"Therefore if any man be in Christ, he is a _____ _____: old things are passed away; behold, all things are become new."*

Welcome the love of God into your heart. When your heart is full of that love, there is no room for the mad dog. Look to Jesus.

- *I Corinthians 13:4–8*— *"Love suffers long and is kind; love does not envy; love does not parade itself, is not puffed up; does not behave rudely, does not seek its own, is not provoked, thinks no evil; does not rejoice in iniquity, but rejoices in the truth; bears all things, believes all things, hopes all things, endures all things. Love never fails" (NKJV).*

So, if you find anger barking at your gate, or jumping at your fence, recognize it as the enemy's mad dog. If it's in your yard biting everyone, and you're holding his leash (by your thoughts), STOP. Talk to God. Take God as your partner. March the mad dog out of your yard. Let go of his leash.

Then, shut the gate. Set a watch against the mad dog. Get a better pet. Welcome in the love of God.

Be a Sleuth

Are there situations or substances that make anger easier? Is it easier to get angry when you're tired? Is it easier to get angry when you've had an extra-large meal, spicy foods, lots of sugar, or caffeine? How do health choices make anger easier? What are you going to do about it?

Don't Be Afraid

"What time I am afraid, I will trust in Thee" (Psalm 56:3).

The Bible says to "fear not." BUT, how can I possibly do that when I have all the emotions of fear, anxiety, or worry running around in my body, when my legs are trembling, or my stomach is in "knots," or there is a threatening, troubling, or worrisome situation going on? How can I simply "not fear"?

Fear is natural, even seemingly automatic, when our sense of well-being is threatened. But, our loving God offers us something better—something peaceful—even in the middle of difficulty.

- *John 14:27— "Peace I leave with you, My _____ I give unto you: not as the world giveth, give I unto you. Let not your heart be troubled, neither let it be afraid."*

If we will trust God, He will give us peace.

God doesn't simply tell us "don't be afraid." Many of the places in the Bible that talk about fear also talk about a solution. The Bible gives us two basic things that fragment fear: trust in God, and love. Let's look at what it says.

Trust in God

The Bible gives us many reasons why God can be trusted, and why He *should* be trusted in those times when fear seems natural. Here are a few.

- *Isaiah 41:10— "Fear thou not; for I am _____ thee: be not dismayed; for I am _____ God: I will _____ thee; yea, I will _____ thee; yea, I will _____ thee with the right hand of My righteousness."*

- *Isaiah 12:2— "Behold, God is my _____; I will trust, and not be afraid: for the Lord Jehovah is my strength and my song; He also is become my salvation." (see also Psalm 112:7; Jeremiah 29:11; Romans 5:8; 8:31, 32, 38, 39)*

We must trust that He is helping us, no matter what appearances are. He gave His life for us. He has promised to be with us through life's difficulties. *(Hebrews 13:5, 6)*

We may not understand *how* trust destroys fear, but it's worth a try—a persistent try—isn't it?

In order to gain more trust (faith) in God, we need to daily study God's Word and, of course, obey it.

- *Romans 10:17— "So then faith cometh by hearing, and hearing by the _____ of God." (see also James 1:22; Proverbs 1:33; John 8:32)*

Love

If we fill our hearts with the love of God, and with love for His children, there will be no room for fear.

- *I John 4:18— "There is no fear in _____; but perfect love casteth out fear: because fear hath torment. He that feareth is not made perfect in love." (see also Romans 8:15; II Timothy 1:7)*

Love also shows itself in obedience—faith that works by love and purifies the heart and life.

- *I John 2:5— "But whoso _____ His word, in him verily is the love of God perfected: hereby know we that we are in Him." (see also John 14:15)*

We may not understand exactly *how* love replaces fear, but it's worth our time to allow love to fill our lives. The possibilities are promising.

How do we get more love for God and His children? By looking again and again at how much He has loved us. God will also be delighted to give us more love, if we ask Him to fill our hearts with it.

- *I John 4:19*— *"We love Him, because He _____ loved us." (please also see I John 4:16, 17; II Corinthians 3:18; Hebrews 12:2, 3)*

* * * * * * *

The power and Word of God is effective for the many colors of fear—dark and drab, or very vivid. But no matter the color, fear torments us *(see I John 4:18)*. There is chronic crippling fear, or panic paralyzing fear, or just plain worry. We may not each fear the same thing, or share the same intensity of fear, but for every shade of fear, God has a sunny colored solution.

For the **fear of want,** in all its dusty brown hues, God promises to be with us and to provide for our real needs.

- *Psalm 34:10— "The young lions do lack, and suffer hunger: but they that seek the Lord shall not _____ [lack] any good thing."*

- *Philippians 4:19— "But my God shall supply all your _____ according to His riches in glory by Christ Jesus."*

Even in very troubling times, we can trust our loving Heavenly Father to care for us.

- *Habakkuk 3:17, 18— "_____ the fig tree shall not blossom, neither shall fruit be in the vines; the labour of the olive shall fail, and the fields shall yield no meat; the flock shall be cut off from the fold, and there shall be no herd in the stalls: yet I will _____ in the Lord, I will joy in the God of my salvation." (see also Psalm 37:25; Matthew 6:31–34; Luke 22:35; Hebrews 13:5)*

We need not fear want any more. God will provide for our actual needs. He is faithful.

For the **fear of suffering and death** in its blackish shades, God promises to be with us through it all.

- *Psalm 23:4—* *"Yea, though I walk through the valley of the shadow of death, I will fear no evil: for Thou art _____ me; Thy rod and Thy staff they comfort me."*

- *Revelation 2:10—* *"Fear _____ of those things which thou shalt suffer: behold, the devil shall cast some of you into prison, that ye may be tried; and ye shall have tribulation ten days: be thou faithful unto death, and I will give thee a crown of life." (see also Mark 4:35–41; Luke 12:4–7; II Corinthians 4:8–18; I Peter 4:12–19)*

We need not fear suffering or death any more. God will be with us. We have the hope of the resurrection and eternal life. *(see Job 19:25–27; I Thessalonians 4:13–18)*

For the **fear of failure** in its slimy green colors, God promises His help. He has promised to be with us no matter what happens. *(see Matthew 28:20; Hebrews 13:5)*

In this next verse, Joshua has just been given the leadership of a nation, along with enemy territory to conquer. Notice *why* God tells him not to fear.

- *Joshua 1:9—* *"Have not I commanded thee? Be strong and of a good courage; be not afraid, neither be thou dismayed: for the Lord thy God is _____ thee whithersoever thou goest." (read the story in Joshua 1:1–9)*

When young King Solomon was supposed to build a magnificent temple to God, the Creator, why did he not need to fear failure?

- *I Chronicles 28:20—* *"And David said to Solomon his son, Be strong and of good courage, and do it: fear not, nor be dismayed: for the Lord God, even my God, will be _____ thee; He will not fail thee, nor forsake thee, until thou hast finished _____ the work for the service of the house of the Lord."*

When King Jehoshaphat was facing enemy armies, why was he told not to fear failure?

- *II Chronicles 20:15, 17—* *"Thus saith the Lord unto you, Be not afraid nor dismayed by reason of this great multitude; for the battle is not yours, but _____. … Ye shall not need to fight in this battle: set yourselves, stand ye still, and see the salvation of the Lord with you, O Judah and Jerusalem: fear not, nor be dismayed; to morrow go out against them: for the Lord will be*

_____ you." *(see II Chronicles 20:1–28, and also II Corinthians 9:8–11)*

On a deeper level, fear of failure often seems to be a fear of the results of failure and the consequences that people may inflict on us. God understands about that, too. His Word has wisdom for us. *(see Micah 7:8; Jeremiah 1:8; Matthew 10:26–31)*

We need not fear failure anymore. God will be with us and help us.

We can trust the wisdom, care, and overruling providence of a loving God—in every situation of life.

For all the colors of fear and worry that you face, God has a sunny colored solution. Search the Scriptures for His words of hope.

For all the colors of fear and worry that you face, God has a sunny colored solution. Search the Scriptures for His words of hope.

Be a Sleuth
What is the effect of exercise upon fear? Does time out in nature have any calming effects? What about soothing music?

Fear Fighting Formula

"What time I am afraid, I will trust in Thee" (Psalm 56:3).

So, what do you do when fear is trembling at your door? Try the **Fear Fighting Formula**.

T – R – U – S – T

<u>T</u>ell and <u>T</u>urn
Tell God all about your fears.
- *Psalm 55:22—* "_____ *thy burden upon the Lord, and He shall sustain thee: He shall never suffer the righteous to be moved."*

- *Philippians 4:6, 7— "Be careful for nothing; but in every thing by* _____ *and supplication with thanksgiving let your requests be made known unto God. And the peace of God, which passeth all understanding, shall keep your hearts and minds through Christ Jesus." (see also Hebrews 4:14–16)*

Turn your thoughts—persistently and repeatedly—away from your fears, toward God and His Word.

- *Isaiah 26:3—* *"Thou wilt keep him in perfect peace, whose mind is _____ on Thee: because he trusteth in Thee."*

- *Psalm 91:4—* *"He shall cover thee with His feathers, and under His wings shalt thou _____: His truth shall be thy shield and buckler."*

- *Proverbs 30:5—* *"Every word of God is pure: He is a shield unto them that put their _____ in Him."* *(see also James 4:7; II Corinthians 10:3–5)*

<u>R</u>epeat Scripture

Jesus repeated scripture when facing life's troubles. We should follow His example. *(see Matthew 4:1–11; Hebrews 4:12)*

In order for you to remember and repeat scripture when you need it, you will have to memorize it.

- *Psalm 17:4—* *"Concerning the works of men, by the _____ of Thy lips I have kept me from the paths of the destroyer."*

- *Psalm 119:11—* *"Thy word have I _____ in mine heart, that I might not sin against Thee."*

Especially memorize and repeat those scriptures that talk about God's love, His faithfulness, and His tender care. Also find those texts that specifically apply to your particular situation.

<u>U</u>nderstand God's Love

It's for you—it's to share. More of God's love in = more fear out.

- *I John 4:18—* *"There is no fear in love; but perfect love _____ _____ fear: because fear hath torment. He that feareth is not made perfect in love."* *(see also John 3:16; Ephesians 3:17–19)*

<u>S</u>ing and <u>S</u>mile

Yes, try singing a thankful, faith–filled hymn—despite your emotions. Eventually the feelings will catch up with the faith. You'd be surprised how helpful it is.

- *Psalm 69:30— "I will praise the name of God with a _____, and will magnify Him with _____ _____."*

- *Proverbs 15:13— "A _____ heart maketh a cheerful countenance: but by sorrow of the heart the spirit is broken." (see also Colossians 3:16, 17)*

A whole army tried it as they went to battle. We should try it for our battles, also. (*II Chronicles 20:15, 21, 22—read the whole story in II Chronicles 20:1–30*)

Paul and Silas tried it in prison. (*Acts 16:22–26*)

It's effective!

<u>T</u>rust

Trust God's care and personal interest in you.

- *Romans 8:28— "And we know that _____ things work together for good to them that love God, to them who are the called according to His purpose."*

- *I Peter 5:7— "Casting all your care upon Him; for He _____ for you." (see also Psalm 55:22; II Peter 1:2–4; II Corinthians 9:8; Deuteronomy 20:3, 4)*

So, when fear is trembling at your door, or in your heart, remember the fear fighting formula:

T – R – U – S – T.

Tell and Turn. Repeat Scripture. Understand God's Love. Sing and Smile. Trust.

And, always remember this helpful verse.

- *Psalm 34:4 —"I sought the Lord, and He heard me, and _____ me from all my fears."*

Be a Sleuth

How much happier would we be if these instructions were set to work in every situation of life? Starting now?

I'm Good

Pride is a "disease" that tends to fasten itself on us the most just when are starting to do well. Yes, and it comes to us when we look good, dress well, own some nice things, or finally accomplish something. But it is a pesky thing that hides Jesus, doesn't treat "lessers" nicely, and blinds us to our own sins and problems. What are we to do about it?

Let's look in God's Word.

- *Jeremiah 9:23, 24—* "Thus saith the Lord, Let not the wise man _____ in his wisdom, neither let the mighty man _____ in his might, let not the rich man _____ in his riches: but let him that glorieth glory in this, that he _____ and _____ Me, that I am the Lord which exercise lovingkindness, judgment, and righteousness, in the earth: for in these things I delight, saith the Lord."

It's not just the empty, cheap, or bad things that we aren't to glory in; it's even worthwhile things, and our good accomplishments.

When we understand and know God—His loving-sacrifice, wisdom, and righteousness—*our* stuff, and *our* accomplishments, will seem as small as they truly are.

Furthermore, all we have has come from someone else.

- *I Corinthians 4:7— "For who maketh thee to differ from another? and what hast thou that thou didst not _____? now if thou didst receive it, why dost thou _____, as if thou hadst not received it?"*

That's pretty plain.

And all the things we mere mortals get ourselves puffed up about, are sooner or later going to pass away,
- *I Peter 1:24, 25— "All flesh [humanity] is as grass, and all the _____ of man as the flower of grass. The grass withereth, and the flower thereof falleth away: but the word of the Lord endureth for ever."*

But, when we have done what we are supposed to, shouldn't we pat ourselves on the back?
- *Luke 17:10— "So likewise ye, when ye shall have done _____ those things which are commanded you, say, We are _____ servants: we have done that which was our _____ to do." (see verses 1–19)*

Then, when we think that *finally* we're doing pretty good at getting it all right, here's something to think about.
- *Isaiah 64:6— "All our righteousnesses are as _____ rags." (see also I Corinthians 10:12; Luke 14:11; I Peter 5:5, 6)*

Yes, even the good things that we do can all be done for the wrong reasons. They are corrupted by our sinful selves.

So, instead of exalting ourselves, or getting puffed up, what should we do?
- *I Peter 5:6— "Humble _____ therefore under the mighty hand of God, that He may exalt you in due time."*

Humble yourselves—you, yourself have a work to do in your heart.

Under the mighty hand of God—yield to His way, His will, and His working.

That He may exalt you—God will exalt what needs to be exalted in you—a likeness to Jesus.

In due time—OK, just trust Him.

We poor sinners are so prone to glory in ourselves, but we really have nothing to glory about! Let us glory in Christ alone.

- *Galatians 6:14—* *"But God forbid that I should glory, save in the _____ of our Lord Jesus Christ, by whom the world is crucified unto me, and I unto the world."*

Never forget that pride will soon shrink when we remember that our sins crucified Christ.

> **Be a Sleuth**
> What should you do when you feel pride creeping up on you? What about when he's already strutting around inside your head? Read II Corinthians 10:5. God can fulfill this promise to you!

When Life Seems Overwhelming

"From the end of the earth will I cry unto Thee, when my heart is overwhelmed: lead me to the rock that is higher than I" (Psalm 61:2).

There are many things that can make life seem overwhelming. You can probably make *your* personal list of overwhelming circumstances. What are we to do for the inner life when we can't seem to fix it? Or what about the outer life? When our remedies aren't working, or we don't seem to have access to workable remedies, what are we to do from the bottom of the hole?

The answer *begins* by looking up—looking up to the sympathizing Heavenly Father … looking up to all that Jesus has given of Himself for you. Begin by looking up.

- *Isaiah 45:22—* "_____ *unto Me, and be ye saved, all the ends of the earth: for I am God, and there is none else." (see also Psalm 5:1–3; 56:3; 124; 142; Hebrews 12:1–3; II Corinthians 4:15–18)*

After you have had a thorough look, remember, this self-sacrificing God can be trusted with the care of you and your problems. Nothing is too big for Him; He upholds the universe.

- *Romans 8:32— "He that spared not His own Son, but delivered Him up for us all, how shall He not with Him also _____ give us all things?"*

- *I Peter 5:7— "Casting _____ your care [difficulties] upon Him; for He careth for you." (see also Psalm 55:22)*

- *II Corinthians 12:9— "And He said unto me, My grace is _____ for thee: for My strength is made perfect in weakness. Most gladly therefore will I rather glory in my infirmities, that the power of Christ may rest upon me."*

- *Romans 8:28— "And we know that _____ things work together for good to them that love God, to them who are the called according to His purpose." (see also II Peter 3:9; II Corinthians 9:8)*

God isn't going to remove all difficulties from our lives. The history of the human race is full of troubles and overwhelming events. It's a sinful world. But God sent His Son to this world to live a life of suffering. With a sympathetic heart, He walks beside us in our suffering. God knows; He cares.

- *Hebrews 4:16— "Seeing then that we have a great high priest, that is passed into the heavens, Jesus the Son of God, let us hold fast our profession. For we have not an high priest which cannot be touched with the feeling of our infirmities; but was in _____ points tempted like as we are, yet without sin. Let us therefore come boldly unto the throne of grace, that we may obtain mercy, and find grace to help in time of need." (see also I Peter 2:20–24)*

We can look forward to the time when all suffering will be ended. That will be a glorious day!

- *Revelation 21:1, 4— "And I saw a new heaven and a new earth: for the first heaven and the first earth were passed away; and there was no more sea. ... And God shall _____ _____ all tears from their eyes; and there shall be no more death, neither sorrow, nor crying, neither shall there be any more pain: for the former things are passed away." (see also Isaiah 65:17–19)*

In the meantime, it will do us good to remember that these things are temporary; these things will pass. *(see Psalm 30:5; II Corinthians 4:17, 18; I Peter 4:12, 13)*

In addition, there are some small but powerful things that can help lift our hearts when life seems overwhelming.

Read the Psalms and the Gospels.

Scatter small sprinkles of sunshine in someone's life—especially to those who are worse off than yourself.

- *Proverbs 14:21*— *"He that despiseth his neighbour sinneth: but he that hath mercy on the poor, _____ is he." (see also Isaiah 58:6–11; I Thessalonians 5:14; Luke 6:38)*

Remember how God has provided for you in the past. He will continue to provide for your needs.

- *I Samuel 7:12— "Hitherto hath the Lord helped us."*

- *Psalm 63:7— "Because Thou hast been my help, _____ in the shadow of Thy wings will I rejoice." (see also Psalm 40:1–5; Psalm 46)*

> *"O God, our help in ages past, Our hope for years to come,*
> *Our shelter from the stormy blast, And our eternal home!"*
> *—Isaac Watts (1719)*

Talk thanksgiving and faith—in word and song. This will brighten others' lives, as well as your own. (If you can't sing, just read the hymn-book. It can be very faith-building.)

- *I Thessalonians 5:18— "In _____ thing give _____: for this is the will of God in Christ Jesus concerning you."*

- *Philippians 4:4— "_____ in the Lord alway: and again I say, _____." (see also Philippians 4:6, 7; Colossians 4:2)*

Remember to trust the Hand that was nailed to the cross for you. *(see Isaiah 26:3, 4; Proverbs 16:20; Deuteronomy 33:29; I Peter 1:3–9; Romans 5:1, 2; 8:32, 35–39; Hebrews 2:17, 18; 4:14–16; 10:23)*

Be a Sleuth

How can the following items benefit you, when life seems overwhelming?

Adequate rest—especially before midnight.
Time out—quiet time out in nature.
Lighten up your diet—delete the monster meals and sporadic snacking; add more fresh fruits and veggies.
Exercise—light to moderate, out of doors in the fresh air and sunshine is best—use wisdom.
Water—drinking plenty.
A regular schedule—try to be consistent.
Giving up harmful substances—for good.
Doing something creative—something you enjoy.

God's Plan for Victory

"But thanks be to God, which giveth us the victory through our Lord Jesus Christ"(I Corinthians 15:57).

You may be reading this study because you are, or have been, a captive of some bad habit. Perhaps anger, anxiety, fear, hopelessness, a corrupting thought life, secret sin, pride or other negative life patterns are weighing you down. God plans that through Jesus Christ we may be free—free indeed.

Look at this prophecy about freedom through Christ.
- *Isaiah 61:1— "The Spirit of the Lord God is upon Me; because the Lord hath anointed Me to preach good tidings unto the meek; He hath sent Me to bind up the brokenhearted, to proclaim _____ to the captives, and the opening of the prison to them that are bound." (see also Luke 4:16–21; John 8:36)*

Christ came to set us at liberty! Freedom from damaging habits and negative thinking patterns can be ours, through Jesus. He can free us from everything that weighs us down.
- *Hebrews 12:1, 2— "Wherefore seeing we also are compassed about with so great a cloud of witnesses, let us lay aside*

God's Plan for Victory | 103

_____ *weight, and the* _____ *which doth so easily beset us, and let us run with patience the race that is set before us,* _____ *unto* _____ *the Author and Finisher of our faith." (see also Hebrews 4:14–16; Matthew 11:28–30)*

> *Freedom from damaging habits and negative thinking patterns can be ours, through Jesus. He can free us from everything that weighs us down.*

In order to have victory, we must persistently fix our mental gaze upon Jesus! Look at what He promises to those who trust Him for help.

- II Corinthians 9:8— *"And God is able to make all grace abound toward you; that ye, always having all sufficiency in all things, may* _____ *to every good work."*

- II Corinthians 2:14— *"Now thanks be unto God, which always causeth us to* _____ *in Christ, and maketh manifest the savour of His knowledge by us in every place." (see also Ephesians 3:20, 21; I Corinthians 15:57)*

God gives not only forgiveness, but also enabling grace. God's whole loving purpose toward humanity is to save us from the power and effects of sin. *(see John 3:16; II Peter 3:9; Ephesians 2:8–10)*

He even helps us to co-operate with Him.
- *Philippians 2:12, 13— "Wherefore, my beloved, as ye have always obeyed … work out your own salvation with fear and trembling. For it is God which* _____ *in you both to will and to do of His good pleasure."*

Confessing our sinful past to God, and asking forgiveness, is a privilege. Yielding our lives to God's power and His ways is liberty.

So, at the time of temptation, when Satan puts his bad thoughts in your mind, earnestly call out to God for help. He hears. He will strengthen you.

"Do not for a moment acknowledge Satan's temptations as being in harmony with your own mind. Turn from them …" (Ellen White, *Our High Calling*, p. 85).

- *Psalm 138:3*— *"In the day that I cried [prayed] Thou answeredst me, and _____ me with strength in my soul." (see also I Thessalonians 5:17; Psalm 107:13)*

Next, we are to co-operate with God's enabling grace.
- *Galatians 2:20*— *"I am crucified with Christ: nevertheless I live; yet not I, but Christ _____ in me: and the life which I now live in the flesh I live by the faith of the Son of God, who loved me, and gave Himself for me." (see also Ephesians 4:22–24; Colossians 3:1–10; I John 2:5, 6; John 15:5)*

Jesus tells us to consider ourselves dead to the old ways, but alive to God and His ways.
- *Romans 6:11–13*— *"Likewise reckon ye also yourselves to be _____ indeed unto sin, but _____ unto God through Jesus Christ our Lord. Let not sin therefore reign in your mortal body, that ye should obey it in the lusts thereof. Neither yield ye your members [body parts] as instruments of unrighteousness unto sin: but yield yourselves unto God, as those that are alive from the dead, and your members as instruments of righteousness unto God."*

Do not yield yourself—your arms or legs, your brain or tongue, your eyes or ears—to those problem areas of your life! Consider these things to no longer be a part of your life. You are dead to them, and alive to God. Yield yourself to do what is right—to live in God's ways.

If something comes up again ... remember, repeat the right ... repeat, repeat, repeat. Jesus is our never-failing Helper. Keep your eyes on Him. *(see James 4:7, 8; Philippians 2:5; 4:6–8; Hebrews 12:2, 3; Isaiah 26:3; Micah 7:7)*

But what if you get tricked or surprised into falling back into an old habit? Go to Jesus. He still loves you and doesn't condemn you. *(see Jeremiah 31:3; Romans 8:31–39; John 8:11)*

Confess your fall to Him and ask Him to forgive you. Christ is still willing to forgive you and enable victory. Get up!
- *Micah 7:8, 9*— *"Rejoice not against me, O mine enemy: when I fall, I shall _____; when I sit in darkness, the Lord shall be a light unto me. ... He will bring me forth to the light, and I shall behold His righteousness." (see also Luke 15:11–32)*

God's Plan for Victory | 105

Regardless of the pull of the old ways, continue to connect with Christ's work of healing in your life. Continued connection and co-operation with Christ creates conquers. Remember, you are not doing this alone.

Helping the Victory Stick

Here is what to do to help your victory stick.
- *Romans 13:14—* "But _____ ye on the Lord Jesus Christ, and make not provision for the flesh, to fulfil the lusts thereof."

Put on the Lord Jesus Christ—Keep up that constant living connection with Christ through daily Bible study and prayer. *(see John 8:31; 15:4)*

Each morning commit yourself—all that you are, and all that you do—to God. He is able to keep you from falling.
- *Jude 24—* "Now unto Him that is able to _____ you from falling, and to present you faultless before the presence of His glory with exceeding joy." (see also II Timothy 1:12; Philippians 1:6; I Thessalonians 5:24; II Corinthians 9:8; Isaiah 26:12; see also Steps to Christ, p. 70.1, by Ellen White)

Make not provision—Make no allowance for the old ways. None *(see James 4:7, 8)!* Keep nothing that goes with the old ways. Repeatedly reject the old thoughts. Refuse to put yourself in tempting situations. If temping or negative thoughts arise, refuse to dwell on them, or they will become irresistible. Do not yield to it. *(see James 1:14, 15)*

Then, what is bad must be conquered and replaced with what is good.
- *Romans 12:21—* "Be not overcome of evil, but _____ evil with good."

Think about better things.
- *Philippians 4:8—* " Finally, brethren, whatsoever things are _____, whatsoever things are _____, whatsoever things are _____, whatsoever things are _____, whatsoever things are _____, whatsoever things are of _____ _____; if there be any _____, and if there be any _____, think on these things."

Fill your mind with the promises of God's Word.
Memorize. Review. Recite.
- *II Peter 1:4—* "Whereby are given unto us exceeding great and precious promises: that by these ye might be _____

of the divine nature, having _____ the corruption that is in the world through lust."

Quote Scripture in the face of temptation, like Jesus did. *(see Matthew 4:1–11; Psalm 17:4; 107:20; 119:11)*

If throughout the day we are memorizing a Bible verse, humming a hymn, or thinking about a Bible passage, the old ways will find less space available in our heads and lives. Persist, and the old ways will get weaker.

Through Jesus the victory is yours.

Be a Sleuth
What health choices will help us to get and to keep the victory?

Prayer

"Continue in prayer, and watch in the same with thanksgiving" (Colossians 4:2).

Prayer is the opening of the heart to God as to a friend. The Creator of the universe invites us to talk to Him as the loving, caring Heavenly Father that He is. He wants to hear from each of us about our lives. That is quite a privilege! *(see Matthew 6:9; Hebrews 4:15, 16)*

There are lots of things that we can pray to God about:

Keep your wants, your joys, your sorrows, your cares, and your fears before God. You cannot burden Him; you cannot weary Him. He who numbers the hairs of your head is not indifferent to the wants of His children. 'The Lord is very pitiful, and of tender mercy' (James 5:11). His heart of love is touched by our sorrows and even by our utterances of them. Take to Him everything that perplexes the mind. Nothing is too great for Him to bear, for He holds up worlds, He rules over all the affairs of the universe. Nothing that in any way concerns our peace is too small for Him to notice. There is no chapter in our experience too dark for Him to read; there is no perplexity too difficult for Him to unravel. No calamity can befall the least of His children, no anxiety harass the soul, no joy cheer, no sincere prayer escape the lips, of which our heavenly Father is unobservant, or in which He takes no immediate interest. 'He healeth the broken in heart, and bindeth up their wounds' (Psalm 147:3). The relations between God and each soul are as distinct and full as though there were not another soul upon the earth to share His watchcare, not another soul for whom He gave His beloved Son. (Ellen White, *Steps to Christ,* p. 100)

He truly is a kind, loving, heavenly Father.
Here are some Bible examples of things to talk to God about.
Praise and Thanksgiving—for who God is, for what He has done, for what He is doing, and for what He has promised to do. (*Psalm 34:1; 63:3; 71:8; 107:1, 2; Isaiah 25:1*)

Confession—admitting my fault, taking full responsibility. I must not justify myself, deny a problem, or blame someone else. (*I John 1:9; Psalm 32:5; 51:3*)

Supplication—earnest and humble requests. (*Philippians 4:6; Psalm 51:1, 2, 7–10; Matthew 7:7–11; 21:22*)

Intercession—asking help for someone else. (*Numbers 14:19; Daniel 9:4–19; Ephesians 6:18; I John 5:14–16*)

Communication—telling God your thoughts. (*I Peter 5:7; Psalm 62:8; 55:22; Philippians 4:6, 7*)

For Christ's sample prayer, *see Matthew 6:9–13.*
Furthermore, prayer is more than just something useful: it is a necessity. Jesus, the Son of God, spent whole nights in prayer. We should develop an unbroken communion with God through prayer.

- *I Thessalonians 5:17— "Pray without _____."*

- *Philippians 4:6, 7— "Be careful for nothing; but in _____ _____ by prayer and supplication with thanksgiving let your requests be made known unto God. And the peace of God, which passeth all understanding, shall keep your hearts and minds through Christ Jesus."*

God is very willing to respond to our heartfelt prayers.
- *Matthew 7:11— "If ye then, being evil, know how to give good gifts unto your children, how much _____ shall your Father which is in heaven give good things to them that ask Him?"* (see also Jeremiah 33:3; Ephesians 3:20, 21; Psalm 107:20)

Even when we don't know exactly what to pray, the Holy Spirit will make intercession for us. We can trust putting ourselves into the kind Heavenly Father's hands.

- *Romans 8:26, 27—* *"Likewise the Spirit also _____ our infirmities: for we know not what we should pray for as we ought: but the Spirit itself maketh intercession for us with groanings which cannot be uttered. And He that searcheth the hearts knoweth what is the mind of the Spirit, because He maketh intercession for the saints according to the will of God."*

Sometimes when we are dealing with our own negative thought patterns and behaviors that need healing, we don't know exactly what to pray. When that happens, we can pray for God to lead us, by His Word and His Holy Spirit, into the path of obedience and inner peace.

- *Psalm 139:23, 24—* *"Search me, O God, and know my heart: try me, and know my thoughts: and see if there be any wicked way in me, and _____ me in the way everlasting." (John 16:13, 14; Psalm 27:11; 43:3; 109:22–27; 119:105; 143:8)*

Then we can yield to God's way and leave everything in His hands.

- *Matthew 26:39—* *"O my Father, if it be possible, let this cup pass from Me: nevertheless not as I _____, but as Thou wilt." (see also Romans 8:28)*

Go to Jesus when you are broken and sorry. Ask for His forgiveness and cleansing. He always hears those kinds of prayers.

Yet, if we *cling* to known sin in our lives, God won't hear our prayers. We must be willing to give up self and yield ourselves to our loving Creator and His ways.

- *Psalm 66:18—* *"If I regard iniquity in my _____, the Lord will not hear me."*

Does this mean that only "good" people can pray? No! The Bible, from beginning to end, tells of God's plan to save sinners. He even gives us repentance. We cannot save ourselves. We must come to Him.

- *I John 1:9—* *"If we confess our sins, He is faithful and just to _____ us our sins, and to _____ us from all unrighteousness." (see also Acts 5:31)*

Go to Jesus when you are broken and sorry. Ask for His forgiveness and cleansing. He always hears those kinds of prayers.

There is a story in *Luke 18:10–14* about a "good" guy and a "bad" guy and the prayers they prayed. Take a moment to read it—you will find it interesting.

Here are some great promises about God hearing our prayers when we co-operate with His program.

- *I John 5:14—* "And this is the _____ that we have in Him, that, if we ask any thing according to His _____, He heareth us."

- *I John 3:22—* "And whatsoever we ask, we receive of Him, because we _____ His commandments, and do those things that are pleasing in His sight."

- *John 15:7—* "If ye _____ in Me, and My _____ abide in you, ye shall ask what ye will, and it shall be done unto you."

- *John 14:13, 14—* "And whatsoever ye shall ask in My _____, that will I do, that the Father may be glorified in the Son. If ye shall ask any thing in My name, I will do it."

Look at this promise!

- *Hebrews 4:14–16—* "Seeing then that we have a great high priest, that is passed into the heavens, _____ the Son of God, let us hold fast our profession. For we have not an high priest which cannot be touched with the feeling of our infirmities; but was in all points tempted like as we are, yet without sin. Let us therefore come boldly unto the throne of grace, that we may obtain mercy, and find grace to help in time of need."

We can come to our never-failing Heavenly Helper in gratitude for the awesome privilege of prayer.

Be a Sleuth

Why is the great God of the universe willing to listen to *our* prayers?

Be Thankful Still

"In every thing give thanks: for this is the will of God in Christ Jesus concerning you" (I Thessalonians 5:18).

In *everything* give thanks? Be thankful anyway? even though …? Yes, honestly. Thankfulness is a powerful gift God offers for healing and deliverance.

Thankfulness is a practical thing. It is a fluffy jacket to keep your heart warm and happy, even on the chilliest of days. Yes, some days are chilled with troubles, or the cold rain of sorrows, or the winter wind of want, or frosty words, or any number of other cold, dreary, gray clouds. We may take any or all of these things to God. He has a compassionate heart, and a listening ear, for troubles, great or small. *(see I Peter 5:7; Psalm 55:22)*

We may be thankful still.

- I Thessalonians 5:18— "In _____ _____ give _____: for this is the will of God in Christ Jesus concerning you."

This may seem outrageous or impossible, but the potential of thanks to lift the heart is worth the effort. God is very willing and able to give us this attitude of gratitude. *(see Isaiah 61:3)*

And in every situation we face, we can be assured that God has only our best interest in mind.

- *Jeremiah 29:11— "For I know the thoughts that I think toward you, saith the Lord, thoughts of _____, and not of evil, to give you an _____ end [a future and a hope]" (NKJV). (see also I Peter 3:12–16)*

God is still on the throne. We can trust the wisdom of His care. Just as nothing could touch Jesus except by God the Father's permission, so nothing can touch us except what God allows.

- *John 19:11— "Jesus answered, Thou couldest have no power at all against Me, except it were _____ thee from above."*

God is more than able to do what He says. He keeps His promises. *(see Romans 4:21; II Timothy 1:12; 4:18)*

So, when God allows something to try our faith, what does He promise?

- *I Corinthians 10:13— "There hath _____ temptation taken you but such as is common to man: but God is faithful, who will not suffer [permit] you to be tempted above that ye are able; but will with the temptation also make a way to escape, that ye may be able to _____ it."*

- *II Corinthians 12:9— "My _____ is _____ for thee: for My strength is made perfect in weakness."*

That is something to be thankful about!

What a kind God to weigh and measure everything, to consider all the factors, and to provide for our needs! *(see Philippians 4:19; Psalm 103:13, 14, 17; II Corinthians 9:8)*. We may be stretched a bit by life's challenges and discomforts, but if we go to God for help, He will provide what we need to be faithful, regardless of what may come.

Consider this promise.

- *Romans 8:28, 29— "And we know that _____ things work together for _____ to them that love God, to them who are the called according to His purpose. For whom He did foreknow, He also did predestinate [pre-plan] to be conformed to the _____ [likeness] of His Son."*

God has promised to bring good out of everything. That's cheering.

One of the best benefits of faithfulness to God during trials is character transformation. If faithful, we will come out on the other side more like the loving Jesus. He endured suffering and death to buy our freedom. That's something to be very thankful about! *(see Psalm 119:67, 71; I Peter 4:1, 2, 12–19; 5:10; Hebrews 12:1–4; James 1:2–4)*

Have you ever tried the thankful game? Just say one thankful thing after another, and see how long you can keep going. It works solo, or in a group. Combined with prayer, and a little faith, it's works wonders when life seems overwhelming.

Have you ever tried praying God's promises in thankfulness? It goes something like this: "Kind Heavenly Father, thank you for the promise of _____. Thank you that you are working, although I don't always see it. Thank you ...."

Have you ever tried singing a thankful, faith-filled hymn at times when you don't feel thankful? Experiment, and see what happens to you, and those around you, by the time you finish three or four or even a half-dozen of them.

Try singing songs like these: *Praise Him! Praise Him!*, *He's Able*, *My Faith Looks Up to Thee*, *Count Your Blessings*, *Lily of the Valley*, *'Tis so Sweet to Trust in Jesus*, *O for a Thousand Tongues*, *Tell Me the Story of Jesus*, *Marvelous Grace*, *My Faith Has Found a Resting Place*, *No Not One*, *To God be the Glory*, and many more.

Paul and Silas tried it in prison. *(Acts 16:22–34)*

A whole choir tried it under very unusual circumstances. *(II Chronicles 20:1–30)*

The Psalms show that David tried it.

Why don't you give it a try, too?

Be thankful still.

Be a Sleuth

How does persistent thankfulness affect us when we are sick? Does thankfulness affect how people treat us? Does a thankful heart help us bear pain more easily? Does a thankful mind make life's load seem lighter?

Life's Cup

All of us have things in life that can't be fixed—which are beyond our control. Life can sometimes be difficult and uncomfortable. Sometimes people give us a sour or bitter cup of life to drink. It is not pleasant.

All of us have a cup of response that we fill up. As our thoughts and feelings are filling a cup for others, we are drinking it in ourselves. If we fill our cup with anger, fear, sorrow, or a stream of other negative things, it will harm *us* as well as those we serve it to. Even though these thoughts and feelings may pop into our heads, we do not have to own them.

At the moment of difficulty, we need to seek God for help on how to deal with it. We need to pour out all our troubles and negative responses at the feet of our kind, sympathetic Heavenly Father, who understands all things.

- *I Peter 5:7—* "Casting _____ your care [life's challenges] upon Him; for He _____ for you."

- *Psalm 62:8—* "Trust in Him at all times; ye people: _____ _____ your heart before Him: God is a refuge for us."

We must leave our cares with God … and go on.

- *Philippians 3:13, 14—* "Forgetting those things which are _____, and reaching forth unto those things which *are _____, I press toward the mark for the prize of the high calling of God in Christ Jesus."*

Sure, life is unpleasant at times, even difficult; but we have a kind Heavenly Father who understands and is working out good in every circumstance, for those that love Him.
- *Romans 8:28— "And we know that _____ things work together for _____ to them that love God." (see also Philippians 1:6; 4:19)*

And always remember, our mental and emotional cup will not stay empty. When we must drink from life's disagreeable cup, we must turn our minds away from the problem. Then we must fill our cup of thoughts with Christ's healing thoughts from the Bible. Start repeating scripture to yourself. *(see Isaiah 26:3)*

Jesus and His Word are the fountain of living water, filling the needs of our inner cup.
- *John 4:14— "But whosoever _____ of the water that I shall give him shall never thirst; but the water that I shall give him shall be in him a _____ of water springing up into everlasting life." (see also Colossians 1:27)*

From Christ we may drink the cup of salvation.
- *Psalm 116:13— "I will take the _____ of salvation, and call upon the name of the Lord."*

This includes not only forgiveness, but also a portion of His never-failing cup of victory, poured into our tiny, little, mortal cup.
- *I John 4:4— "Ye are of God, little children, and have _____ them: because greater is He that is _____ you, than he that is in the world." (see also I Corinthians 15:57; II Corinthians 2:14; 9:8)*

Christ drank our cup of suffering, that we might drink His cup of joy. *(see Isaiah 12:2, 3; 53:5; I Corinthians 10:4)*

Jesus wants to fill our inner cup (thoughts and emotions) with so much good that there is no room for the bad. J
- *Romans 15:13— "Now the God of hope _____ you with all _____ and _____ in believing, that ye may abound in hope, through the power of the Holy Ghost."*

- *Ephesians 3:19—* *"To know the love of Christ, which passeth knowledge, that ye might be _____ with all the fullness of God." (see also John 14:30; Philippians 1:11; Romans 12:21)*

Also, fill your cup with thoughts of the love and pity of Christ, assurances of the love of God, the precious promises of the Word, the blessings God gives you each day, the hope of heaven, the privilege of prayer, and many other happy things.
- *Psalm 71:8—* *"Let my mouth be _____ with Thy praise and with Thy honour all the day." (see also Colossians 3:15; Psalm 100:4, 5; I Thessalonians 5:18; Hebrews 12:2, 3)*

Offer a cup of thanksgiving to God, and then offer cups of cheerfulness and kindness to those around you. If Christ fills the cup of your heart by His Spirit, what will fill the cup you offer to others?
- *Galatians 5:22, 23—* *"But the fruit of the _____ is love, joy, peace, longsuffering, gentleness, goodness, faith, meekness, temperance." (see also Psalm 23:5)*

Share the cup of life and blessings.
- *Revelation 22:17—* *"And the Spirit and the bride say, Come. And let him that heareth say, Come. And let him that is _____ come. And whosoever will, let him take the _____ of life freely."*

Be a Sleuth

Take a look at the things that you do throughout the day. What are they filling your inner cup with? What kinds of choices do you need to make about the things that go into your mental cup? (*Isaiah 55:2; Philippians 4:8*)

Bibliography

Signs of the Times, May 15, 1893.

White, Ellen G. *The Desire of Age*. Mountain View, CA: Pacific Press Publishing Association, 1898.

White, Ellen G. *Our High Calling*. Washington, DC: Review and Herald Publishing Association, 1961.

White, Ellen G. *Steps to Christ*. Mountain View, CA: Pacific Press Publishing Association, 1892.

TEACH Services, Inc.
P U B L I S H I N G

We invite you to view the complete
selection of titles we publish at:
www.TEACHServices.com

We encourage you to write us
with your thoughts about this,
or any other book we publish at:
info@TEACHServices.com

TEACH Services' titles may be purchased in
bulk quantities for educational, fund-raising,
business, or promotional use.
bulksales@TEACHServices.com

Finally, if you are interested in seeing
your own book in print, please contact us at:
publishing@TEACHServices.com

We are happy to review your manuscript at no charge.

www.ingramcontent.com/pod-product-compliance
Lightning Source LLC
Chambersburg PA
CBHW040315170426
43196CB00020B/2935